Theos
The public theology think tank

C000148366

what Theos is

Theos is a public theology think tank which exists to undertake research and provide commentary on social and political arrangements. The word, "Theos", and our descriptor, "the public theology think tank", reflect our overall aim of putting God "back" into the public domain. Theos is about social, public theology; about public wisdom.

what Theos stands for

Faith is on the public agenda in a way that is unprecedented in recent times. Theos aims to shape events, not simply react to them. Our aim is to speak wisdom into the increasingly crowded market place of ideas. We seek to demonstrate that religion can have a positive role to play in public debate and the communities we seek to serve.

what Theos works on

Theos undertakes research on a wide range of subject areas. We believe that every issue is a moral issue and reject notions of a sacred/secular divide.

what Theos provides

Theos provides:

high-quality research, reports and publications;

an events' programme (including public debates, an annual Theos lecture and an extensive fringe programme at the party conferences);

news, information and analysis to media companies and other opinion-formers, with a one-stop information line available to journalists; and

an informative website, www.theosthinktank.co.uk

In addition to our independently driven work, Theos provides research, analysis and advice to individuals and organisations across the private, public and not-for-profit sectors. Our unique position within the think tank sector means that we have the capacity to develop proposals that carry values - with an eye to demonstrating what really works. Our staff and consultants have strong public affairs experience, an excellent research track record and a high level of theological literacy. We are practised in campaigning, media relations, detailed policy development and effecting policy change.

Published by Theos in 2008
© Theos

ISBN: 978-0-9554453-3-0

For further information and subscription details, please contact:

Theos
Licence Department
34 Buckingham Palace Road
London
SW1W 0RE
United Kingdom

T 020 7828 7777
E hello@theosthinktank.co.uk
www.theosthinktank.co.uk

Neither Private nor Privileged

The Role of Christianity in Britain Today

by Nick Spencer
foreword by Jim Wallis

contents

acknowledgements

This essay, like its predecessor *Doing God*, has benefited enormously from the insight and wisdom of many people.

My colleagues at Theos, Paul Woolley, Paul Bickley and Jennie Pollock have been as helpful and supportive as ever, as have a number of Theos interns, in particular, Rachel Banting, Rebecca Carpenter, Faith Pilgrim, Francis Murphy and Victoria Thorpe.

Regular comments from the Theos advisory group - David Coffey, Alison Le Cornu, Owenna Griffiths, James Hanvey, Ann Holt, Rob Hutton, Danny Kruger, David Landrum, Anna Robbins, and Lucy Winkett - have also proved invaluable, as have further comments from those who, whilst having no formal association with Theos, were kind enough to read and comment on various drafts: Jonathan Chaplin, Richard Chartres, Toby Hole, Peter Misselbrook and Graham Tomlin.

Margaret Reece did her usual, forensic job in proofreading, for which I am grateful. It should go without saying that the success or otherwise of the argument within this essay is due to the author alone.

Nick Spencer

The question of the proper role of Christians and the church in relation to public life is one that has occupied much of my work for years. Although the British history and context are decidedly different than those of the U.S., the challenge of navigating between theocracy on the one hand and a privatized faith in a secular society on the other is very real in both.

The inaugural report from Theos in 2006 argued that religious groups would play a significant role in British public life in the 21st century but did not describe that role. *Neither Private nor Privileged* takes the next step. Positing that the role of the church is to be a "public witness", it argues that the extent to which the state promotes the "public good" should determine the nature of the church's response.

A helpful discussion of Acts chapters 1-5 provides four methods by which the early church engaged in the public square - proclamation, assembly, action, confrontation. The examination of Anglicanism (through the writings of Archbishop Rowan Williams), the Free Churches, and Roman Catholicism finds that, with nuanced differences, each teaches a model that fits these four methods.

The heart of the report is its analysis that the specific actions the church should take depend on the nature of the state - that the closer its moral orientation is to the gospel, the greater the capacity for cooperation. The church therefore has the obligation to closely examine the moral orientation of the state, how its policies and actions contribute to the public good, not religious belief; and measure them against the church's conception of the public good that underlies its public witness. This provides the framework to determine the appropriate response.

As Christians, our ultimate allegiance is always to the kingdom of God. And because the kingdom is not born of worldly kingdoms, biblical politics resists the notion of ideal societies and instead focuses on specific issues and reforms. If our starting point is the kingdom of God, we should reject allegedly utopian or perfect societies, which are impossible creations for sinful people in a fallen world. We should rather seek concrete reforms of the social situations and circumstance in which the church finds itself. We should challenge societies and states with specific demands that make justice and peace more possible. The kingdom is the vision, but concrete political priorities and policies bring us closer to it or farther away from it.

And, as the report correctly points out, for Christians a commitment to the kingdom mandates that we seek the "common good" of the societies in which we live. Catholic social teaching is rich with the idea of the common good, as are Protestant traditions with their idea of the "public good". Black church history is filled with a faith that cared for the whole community when nobody else did. Evangelical revivals led to social reforms and transformed both American and British society. And the common good is not simply a concept embedded within the Christian tradition. Jewish concepts of *shalom* and *tikkun* are about the common good, and the idea is rooted deep in the history and theology of Islam.

The common good suggests that the good of each individual is necessarily and vitally connected to the good of all. It is a test for all the key questions that we face: from family values to foreign policy, from the housing we dwell in to the social values that dwell within us, from health care to healing of our national fears and divisions, from the distribution of our resources to determining the things we value most, from the things that make for peace on a global level to the community level, from our definitions of justice to our practice of it, from what we'd like to change to what gives us hope for ever changing it. Whenever we deal with social and economic decisions and policies, we will always ask what is of the greatest benefit to the common good. We must consider values, right and wrong, and the ways of sustaining or restoring the healthy social and moral fabric of a society.

Neither Private nor Privileged concludes: "Christianity is a public religion and nothing is going to change the Christian imperative to public proclamation, public assembly, public action, and, if necessary, public confrontation. However, the precise role that Christianity plays within the public square can and does change. This report has argued that it will and should change according to its ability to articulate and realize an understanding of and contribution to the public good that sufficiently persuades the public."

It is a conclusion that I heartily support.

Jim Wallis is author of *Seven Ways to Change the World: Reviving Faith and Politics* and president of Sojourners.

privilege and privatisation

"Should religious people have a privileged position in society?"

So asked John Humphrys on Thursday, 19 April 2007, as the *Today* programme drew to a close.[1] The *Mail on Sunday* columnist, Peter Hitchens, and the Labour Peer, Lord Harrison, argued for four and a half minutes. Then *In Our Time* started.

What, you may ask, did they have to say? The answer is obvious. No, they should not. End of debate. 270 seconds saved.

Should religious people have a privileged position in society? The question is all but rhetorical. Privilege is anathema to us today. It is, almost by definition, something of which we disapprove. Of course religious people should not have a privileged position in society. *Nobody* should have a privileged position in society.

The real question is: what constitutes privilege? In the *Today* debate, Lord Harrison cited the lack of any "representative from the non-religious community" at the Cenotaph on Remembrance Day, the existence of hospital, army and prison chaplains, and the *Today* programme's very own "Thought for the Day".

In a House of Lords debate on the topic later that day he added the establishment of the Church of England, the selection process of certain "faith" schools, prayers in Parliament, the fact that humanist marriage ceremonies are not recognised as legal, and Radio 4's two-minute "Prayer for the Day" ("I deplore the abuse of that unearned licence as the nation's reveille at 5.45 am").[2]

> *The real question is: what constitutes privilege?*

Surprisingly, he made no mention of the presence of 26 bishops in the Lords, the blasphemy laws or the nature of the Coronation. Nor did he cite the supposedly compulsory act of worship in schools, Christmas and Easter public holidays, the presence of a cross on the Union Jack, the existence of patron saints, the words of the National Anthem, the inscription on British coins or the laws limiting Sunday trading. If this long list does not constitute privilege for religious, meaning effectively Christian, groups, what does?

common ground

Theos was launched in November 2006. Its inaugural essay was entitled *Doing God* and argued that, Alistair Campbell notwithstanding, there *was* a future for "faith" in the public square. Beyond the rise of aggressive, political Islam, the best-known theo-political phenomenon of our age, *Doing God* argued that there were a number of more positive reasons why religious groups would play a significant role in British public life in the twenty-first century. The return of civil society, the emerging political interest in well-being and the growth of identity politics all point towards a greater role for God in the public square. These, combined with problems facing the intellectual foundations of liberal humanism, and the basic demographic fact that wherever they are found religious groups "out-breed" non-religious ones, suggest that we would see rather more religious engagement in British public life than had, until recently, been confidently predicted.[3]

Doing God did not, however, attempt to outline *what* that engagement should look like. Beyond gesturing in the direction of some of the challenges that "doing God" demands, it did not describe what role religion should actually play in British public life.

Neither Private nor Privileged attempts to do that, although with some apprehension. Writing in the *Guardian* in February 2007, Stuart Jeffries observed:

> Britain is dividing into intolerant camps who revel in expressing contempt for each other's most dearly held beliefs ... Britain's new cultural divide is not between Christian and Muslim, Hindu and Jew. It is between those who have faith and those who do not.[4]

He is not alone in sensing the rising temperature of the debate about religion in general and religious influence in public life in particular. On the one hand, a series of eloquent and angry atheist polemics by respected public intellectuals has helped legitimise contempt towards religious belief.[5] On the other, some religious believers have resorted to rather incendiary similes to get their message across,[6] whilst others have become increasingly willing to turn to the courts to defend their alleged rights,[7] and still others have made aggressive, and even criminal public protests against art they deemed blasphemous.[8]

Such a febrile mood does not augur well for an attempt to outline the role of religious belief in the public square. Even assuming that respective parties were able to locate any common, consensual ground, it seems unlikely that they would want to share it.

public good

And yet, as *Doing God* argued, the issue of religious participation in the public square is not going to go away in the way that sociologists once predicted.[9] Simply to ignore the issue would be to cede ground to those who wish to turn conversation into controversy, and controversy into conflict.

More pointedly, the issue of religious participation in the public square is here to stay because it is part of a broader ineradicable question relating to the moral orientation of the state. Under what concept(s) of public good are we living?

The question may at first seem odd, living as we do in a liberal state that prides itself on *not* imposing any conception of the good upon its citizens. Yet, the truly neutral state is a chimera. However much we might attempt to privatise life - whether through the adoption of human rights or the extension of market mechanisms into every aspect of life - shared public "space" is an irreducible phenomenon, and public space that is not simply anarchy must be governed by some idea of public good. Whether it is in terms of actual physical space, or of money, time or legislation, we still live *together*, and whether or not we share values some are still "imposed" on us by simple virtue of our cohabitation. Where should public money be spent? What criteria should be adopted for regulating markets? How should the Charity Commission define "public benefit"? How should we protect our shared natural environment? How should policymakers evaluate the worth of public services?[10] Which days should be made public holidays? What public good does the BBC serve? Our answers to such questions, many of which rank among the most important and far-reaching in contemporary Britain, reveal our concept of the public good, and in particular, how far that concept is informed by various cultural, philosophical and religious commitments. It is this question - of what notion of the good, what "moral orientation," shapes our public life - that underpins any discussion of what role Christianity should play in it.

Unlike *Doing God, Neither Private nor Privileged* focuses not on religion in general, but on Christianity in particular. The reason for this is that, whilst the trends identified in *Doing God* relating to civil society, well-being and identity apply to most religions, the subsequent question of what role each should play in the public square will depend on different theological perspectives, and historical, cultural and demographic contingencies. Generalisations about "religion" are liable to cloud rather than clarify the issue.

> The issue of religious participation in the public square is not going to go away.

The essay is divided into five chapters. The first lays out the range of possible roles for Christianity in the public square, from the minimal (i.e. faith is privatised) to the maximal (i.e. we live in a theocracy). It deals only briefly with the first position, referring readers to a more detailed discussion in chapter 1 of *Doing God*, and focuses, instead, on the second. The accusation that Christian engagement in the public square naturally tends towards theocracy stands somewhere close to the heart of most secular arguments against mixing religion and public life - and with good reason. The history of Christian engagement with political power is not an entirely happy one and no one advocating Christian involvement in the public square can afford to be complacent about how wrong it can go. That said, chapter 1 argues that there are good reasons to believe that Western Christianity's theocratic temptation has been overcome, partly through a rediscovery of the New Testament's attitude to the state, and partly through the bitter experience of history. The oft-cited counter example, would-be theocratic America, is in fact nothing of the sort, as chapter 1 explains.

> *The history of Christian engagement with political power is not an entirely happy one.*

Chapter 2 explores the gap between the poles described in chapter 1 by asking what contemporary Christians are actually advocating for Christian public engagement. If neither privatisation nor theocracy is a sound or attractive option, what is, in fact, on the table? What do the UK's leading Christian figures and denominations advocate for the Church's engagement in public life? The chapter argues that the earliest Church, as described in the first five chapters of St Luke's Acts of the Apostles, had a four-fold pattern of public engagement, consisting of public proclamation, public assembly, public action and public confrontation. It goes on to argue that this four-fold structure, described by the umbrella term of "public witness", offers a good way of analysing what the main UK Christian traditions - Anglicanism, the Free Churches and Roman Catholicism - advocate for Christianity's role in the public square.

> *The Church needs to be able to respond to the nature of the state in which it finds itself.*

Chapter 3 takes this idea of Christianity as a form of "public witness" and asks what might that actually entail? The fact that Rowan Williams and Norman Kember, the peace activist seized in Iraq, are both technically engaged in the activity of "public witness" indicates how broad the term is. What form of "public witness" should Christianity adopt in modern Britain? In particular, should Christianity act as a witness within, without or even against official public structures?

This chapter goes on to argue that, rather than offering a conclusive answer to this question, Christian Scripture and tradition advocate flexibility. Whilst there are principles for the way in which the Church should engage with the state, there is no blueprint outlining, for example, whether it must be established, participate in the legislature, work with public money, or advocate civil disobedience. Certain boundaries, such as privatisation on the one hand and theocracy on the other, should not be crossed, and certain principles should be observed. But the fundamental idea is that the Church needs to be able to respond to the nature of the state in which it finds itself.

This is where the concept of the public good comes in. Put bluntly, if a state's concept of public good is very different from that of the gospel, the Church will naturally find itself working outside or even against official structures. The state, in effect, will have excluded the Church, which will thenceforth operate in the Norman Kember mode of public witness, rather than, say, the Rowan Williams one. If, on the other hand, the state's concept of the good is much closer to the gospel's, the Church may legitimately operate alongside or even within official structures.

It is a basic Christian belief that no state will ever truly embody gospel values and it is a basic historical fact that very few will ever be totally at odds with them. Even the idolatrous Roman Empire was recognised by New Testament writers for its duty to punish wrongdoers and restrain evil. The task, then, is to understand the notion of public good embodied by the state in question. This is the focus of chapter 4, which explores this notion of public good, this "moral orientation", of the British state.

This, it recognises, is a difficult task and not simply because British society itself is morally plural - the chapter makes it clear that the moral orientation of a state is not the same thing as that of its population. Rather, it is difficult for two specific reasons, one relating to the inheritance of previous concepts of public good that are not necessarily shared today, and the other relating to the necessary fudges and compromises, and the frequent lack of joined-up thinking that can characterise modern policymaking. The result is that it is better to talk of the state's moral orientations, in the plural, and to advocate a case-by-case approach to the role of Christianity in modern British public life.

Chapter 5 recaps this argument and contends that, even though the path to this conclusion covers theological ground, the conclusion itself is not explicitly theological or, indeed, premised on any particular ideological commitments, and thus, should hopefully persuade those who do not share the same, or indeed any theological convictions. It then concludes by briefly sketching out, with several examples, what the essay's argument would mean for evaluating the role of Christianity in the public square.

Those reading *Neither Private nor Privileged* for a comprehensive or definitive analysis of the role of Christianity in modern Britain will be disappointed. The very essence of its argument is that those who call for simple, sweeping action in this area fail to do justice to an extremely complex issue. A more cautious, case-by-case analysis is needed, for which *Neither Private nor Privileged* offers a framework.

Thus, if *Doing God* described itself as a rubble clearing exercise, an attempt "to clear away some of the objections against letting God into the public square and to create a space for public theology", *Neither Private nor Privileged* sees itself as a foundation sinking one. It offers a framework for subsequent analysis of the role of Christianity in the British public square, one that is based, ultimately, on the extent to which, by doing what it must do, Christianity can persuade the public that it is "doing good".

It is hoped that the framework will be accessible and credible to non-Christians as well as Christians, and that it will provide a basis for subsequent, more specific explorations of the role of Christianity in the public square. It is under no illusions about how tense and acrimonious that debate is becoming, but it is hoped that it may, in some small way, help steer it from conflict and controversy back towards conversation.

introduction - references

1   The debate can be heard at http://www.bbc.co.uk/radio4/today/listenagain/zthursday_20070419.shtml

2   Lord Harrison, Hansard, 19 April 2007, columns 331-34

3   For a very brief survey of the various intellectual threats to liberal humanism, see Nick Spencer, *Doing God: A Future for Faith in the Public Square* (Theos, 2006), pp. 67-68. For the demographic trends of religious and non-religious groups, see Eric Kaufmann, "Breeding for God", *Prospect*, November 2006, http://www.prospect-magazine.co.uk/article_details.php?id=7913

4   Stuart Jeffries, "Faith", the *Guardian*, 26 February 2007

5   See, for example, Richard Dawkins, *The God Delusion* (Transworld, 2006); Christopher Hitchens, *God is not Great: The Case against Religion* (Atlantic, 2007); Sam Harris, *Letter to a Christian Nation: A Challenge to the Faith of America* (Bantam, 2007); AC Grayling, *Against all Gods: Six Polemics on Religion and an Essay on Kindness* (Oberon Books, 2007)

6   Thus, Cardinal Keith O'Brien described the rate of abortion in Scotland as the equivalent to "two Dunblane massacres a day"

7   For example, Lydia Playfoot and the Silver Ring Thing; the Christian Union at Exeter University; the Bishop of Hereford and John Reaney; Aishah Azmi and the Church of England School at which she worked in Dewsbury; Shabina Begum and the school she attended in Luton; the case of an unnamed 12-year-old Muslim school girl and her Buckinghamshire school. It is only fair to note the religious individual or organisation was not always the litigant in these cases

8   For example, some Christians who persuaded the cancer charity Maggie's Centres to turn down a £3,000 donation that came from the show *Jerry Springer - The Opera;* some Sikhs who successfully closed down the play *Behzti* at The Birmingham Repertory Theatre; and some Muslims who demonstrated against the Danish cartoons of Mohammed with placards saying things like "butcher those who mock Islam" and "Europe you will pay, your 9/11 is on the way"

9   Most famously, Peter Berger who, in the *New York Times* in 1968, forecast that "[by] the twenty-first century, religious believers are likely to be found only in small sects, huddled together to resist a worldwide secular culture", only to write in his 1999 book *The Desecularisation of the World*, "the assumption that we live in a secularised world is false: The world today, with some exceptions … is as furiously religious as it ever was, and in some places more so than ever"

10 For further exploration of this interesting question, see The Work Foundation's project on public value (www.theworkfoundation.com)

the theocratic temptation

The threat of theocracy hangs over us all.

Whether it is the established theocracy of Iran, the emerging theocracy of Turkey, the alleged theocracy of America, or the embryonic theocracy of Madagascar, the world is going to the gods.[1]

"I start from the position that theocracy is one of the least desirable of all forms of political organisation," wrote the author Philip Pullman in the *Guardian* in November 2004.[2]

Few, at least in Britain, would disagree. Theocracy, with its narrow-minded intolerance of "the other" represents everything the West has emerged from and struggled against. It is, we are told, the sole mode of political engagement with which religious groups are actually happy. And in some form or other, it is the ultimate cost of permitting religious conviction into the public square.

> The world is going to the gods.

"Why should the Catholic church seek to impose its beliefs on the rest of us?" entreated the *Guardian's* Jackie Ashley, in the wake of various Catholic bishops' comments on abortion.[3] "It is time to demand ... a right for the rest of us to non-interference by religious persons and organisations," wrote the philosopher AC Grayling in a similar vein, "a right to be free of ... the efforts of self-selected minority groups to impose their own choice of morality and practice on those who do not share their outlook."[4] "When religious groups demand respect, what starts off as a demand for tolerance can rapidly end up as a demand to take over your life," wrote Simon Blackburn in the *Independent.*[5]

There is a lot of rhetoric in all this. "Religions have far more to do with stoning homosexuals than with social welfare provision or affordable housing," Blackburn tells us. Religious people - that oddly opaque, fist-shaking, gay-bashing, book-burning, eco-trashing, vanishingly-small yet ominously-growing group of moral inadequates - threaten to drag us all back to the Middle Ages. We need to wake up, rescue the Enlightenment and put religion back where it belongs: in the privacy of the home.

Beneath such rhetoric, there is some substance. As *Doing God* acknowledged, there *are* some good reasons why we might wish to keep religious conviction from the public square. When Simon Blackburn writes, "when we come to think of ourselves as Jews, Muslims, Christians and Hindus, [it] will lead to an inevitably sectarian society," he is not simply scaremongering. Religious conviction *can* be exclusive and sectarian, not to mention inflexible, inhuman and inaccessible. Its engagement in the public square *can* fracture public discourse and invest debate with an ultimacy it can ill-afford.

Having noted that, banning certain convictions from public debate simply because they are religious is hardly more attractive. Not only would such a measure run counter to the ideal of toleration that has been the emerging mark of British democracy since the late seventeenth century, but it would also be hugely counter-productive. As Karen Armstrong points out in *The Battle for God*, the best way to encourage fundamentalism is to remove from religious groups a public voice and impose on them a secular agenda that they are unable to contest.[6] Excluding one group from the public square because you do not like its creed or believe it to be a threat is the surest way of further alienating that group.

> *The best way to encourage fundamentalism is to remove from religious groups a public voice and impose on them a secular agenda that they are unable to contest.*

Doing God explored these various arguments relating to the privatisation of religious belief, recognising that those intent on mixing religion and politics need to heed their critics.[7] It concluded, however, that, whilst being coherent, such arguments were not conclusive, and should be seen as checkpoints rather than roadblocks on the route to the public square.

If the case for privatising religious faith fails to convince, however, the opposite one, of making it completely, i.e. compulsorily, public is hardly more attractive.

three flavours of theocracy

The term "theocracy" covers a multitude of sins. Narrowly construed, this "rule of God" would demand something like a direct and continuous theophany, or manifestation of the divine. In reality, the term has always been used loosely. The word, if not the concept, can be traced back to the first century Jewish historian, Josephus, who used it in his defence of Judaism, *Against Apion*:

> There are innumerable differences in the particular customs and laws that are among all mankind, which a man may briefly reduce under the following

heads. Some legislators have permitted their governments to be under monarchies, others put them under oligarchies, and others under a republican form … our legislator [Moses] had no regard to any of these forms, but he ordained our government to be what, by a strained expression, may be termed a theocracy, by ascribing the authority and the power to God, and by persuading all the people to have a regard to him, as the author of all the good things that were enjoyed either in common by all mankind, or by each one in particular…[8]

Josephus' "strained" neologism is also somewhat vague. If a theocracy involved simply "ascribing authority and power to God", it would make many democratic theories, constitutions and states, not least the UK, theocratic. Similarly, "persuading … people to have a regard to [God], as the author of all … good things," sounds more Anglican than Taliban in its ambitions.

Technically, theocracy can come in a number of forms. We most readily understand it as "government by priesthood", hierocracy, in which the people are ruled by those with an official, religious function. Alternatively, there is royal theocracy, sometimes called caesaro-papism, in which the ruling authority is not priestly but rather a secular power that is deemed to be sacred.

The long and varied history of early Israel saw it operate in both these modes (just as, at times, it saw it reject both) but neither reflects the form of theocracy to which Josephus referred in *Against Apion*. His theocracy was founded not so much on structures of government as on the national constitution. This, for Israel, was the Torah, believed to have been given by God and disclosing his will for the tribes he had rescued from slavery. In this way, God ruled his people not so much through the prophets, priests or kings who claimed divine authority (and about whom the Hebrew Bible is often witheringly critical) as through his law, which formed the basis of who his people were and how they should live. Israel's theocracy was not so much rule by king or by priest, as rule by law.

> "You don't need a belief in God to have a theocracy".

It is worth noting, in passing, that theocracies, of whatever flavour, do not need to be theistic, let alone Christian. As Philip Pullman pointed out in the article quoted above, "you don't need a belief in God to have a theocracy".[9] Indeed, some authorities that have demonstrated the most distinctive "theocratic" traits - inerrant scripture, an official interpretation, a sacred priesthood, processes for silencing heretics, the demonisation of outsiders, a dominant teleological view of history - have been deliberately anti-theistic. "The Soviet Union," he observed, "was one of the most thoroughgoing theocracies the world has ever seen, and it was atheist to its marrow."

Whilst one might object to the use of the word "theocracy" to describe Communist Russia - it rather implicates God in a system that was wholly opposed to him - Pullman's observation, and indeed the history of the twentieth century, reminds us that it is not simply Christian or religious groups that suffer from and succumb to the theocratic temptation.

Be that as it may, the question still remains, is theocracy, in its royal, priestly or legal form, the state of affairs that Christian engagement in public affairs naturally tends to or desires?

the theocratic temptation

Historically, the evidence is not encouraging. Christendom is commonly cited as the most obvious example of Christianity's theocratic tendency, an example that is frequently accompanied by lurid details of the Spanish Inquisition or the Albigensian Crusade, as if such exercises in brutality were the only things that happened between the fourth and the eighteenth centuries.

The reality of Christendom was, in fact, rather more complex. The very fact that the Western Church preserved for over 1,000 years the language of Church *and* state reflects the legitimacy that autonomous secular power maintained throughout the Christendom period.[10] The epochal confrontation between Pope Gregory VII and the Holy Roman Emperor, Henry IV, in the 1070s and the less epochal but equally dramatic clash between Archbishop Thomas Becket and King Henry II a century later exposed the angry tension that could accompany this dual focus of authority.

If Christendom was never technically a theocracy, however, it certainly had theocratic tendencies. This tension can be traced back at least to the fifth century theologian, St Augustine. He articulated at great length the distinct objectives and jurisdictions of state and Church, but wavered in his attitude to the use of the state's coercive power in matters of theological dispute and ecclesiastical discipline. Thus, he wrote in a letter to Vincentius, bishop of the schismatic Donatist sect:

> Originally my opinion was that no one should be coerced into the unity of Christ, that we must act only by words, fight only by arguments and prevail by force of reason.[11]

Those opinions changed, however, not so much due to argument as to the evidence that coercion worked. Thus, he argued in his later book *The Correction of the Donatists:*

Why ... should not the Church use force in compelling her lost sons to return, if the lost sons compelled others to their destruction?[12]

The length, breadth and diversity of the Christendom period should warn us against glib generalisations. Nevertheless, the ambiguity we see in Augustine's thinking over this issue helps explain the theocratic atmosphere and crimes of a system that was, in theory at least, non-theocratic.

A clearer example of the theocratic temptation of Christian political engagement can be seen in the thought of the Eastern (latterly Orthodox) Church.[13] This maintained a far closer relationship between Church and state than was ever achieved in the West. According to Eastern theology, monotheism was the model for, and thereby demanded, autocracy. The Christian emperor embodied the power, protection and benevolence of the one true God. He was thus empowered to exercise authority over and on behalf of the Church in a way that the theology (not to mention the collapse of Imperial power) in the West proscribed. The Church thus became deeply embedded in the Imperial and latterly national cultures of Eastern Europe, a fact that is still reflected in the Orthodox tendency to marry ecclesiastical and ethnic identities (a heresy known as phyletism and condemned at the pan-Orthodox Synod of 1872).

It is also worth noting that we should not imagine theocratic temptations to be limited to medieval or non-Reformed Churches. Sixteenth century Geneva under the leadership of John Calvin was not a theocracy, in as much as there was clear delineation between the (civic) Council and the (church) Consistory. However, the Consistory still exercised considerable influence over the Council, which was bound to uphold doctrine and enforce ethical practices among the population.[14] Neighbourliness, generosity, hard-work, thrift, abstinence and fidelity were encouraged, whilst laws against gambling, blasphemy, drunkenness, adultery, wild dancing, bawdy singing and naming children after Catholic saints were passed.[15] The results could be impressive - by 1560 Geneva had one of the lowest rates of illegitimacy ever recorded in Europe - but the experience is unlikely to have been an entirely pleasant one.[16]

against theocracy: theology and history

Such examples offer a powerful and disturbing testimony and appear to give succour to those who claim that as soon as those empowered by Christian conviction find themselves in power, they impose their will on everyone else. Are there any exhibits for the defence?

The answer is "Yes": three. The first relates to Christianity's foundational document and what it has to say about the respective roles of the Church and state.[17]

It is no accident that Christian theocracies and quasi-theocracies have commonly needed to rely on models drawn from the Old rather than the New Testament to justify themselves. Augustine cited the model of the repentant King Nebuchadnezzar in the book of Daniel (chapter 3 verse 29) as "prefiguring" the model Christian emperor who defends the integrity of the faith.[18] Calvin was deeply influenced by the example of Old Testament Israel[19] and reformed England's first king, Edward VI, was constantly identified with Josiah, the reforming boy king of Judah. The state of Israel between the time of David and the Babylonian exile provided a powerful, if not always edifying, example of the unitary, godly state.

The New Testament offers rather less succour to would-be theocrats. Hardly surprisingly, given Jesus' death at the hands of the Roman state and his disciples' distinctly tense relationship with the authorities, the New Testament writers did not envisage the "state" doing the work of the Church.[20]

Nor, however, did they advocate revolution or anarchy, as might have been expected. Rather, and perhaps surprisingly, they insisted that the authorities deserved Christians' respect and obedience. "I urge ... that requests, prayers, intercession and thanksgiving be made ... for kings and all those in authority, that we may live peaceful and quiet lives," Paul wrote to Timothy. (1 Timothy 2.1-2) "Remind the people to be subject to rulers and authorities [and] to be obedient," he told Titus. (Titus 3.1) "Submit yourselves ... to every authority instituted among men: whether to the king, as the supreme authority, or to governors, who are sent by him to punish those who do wrong and to commend those who do right," Peter informed the dispersed audience of his first letter. (1 Peter 2.13-14) The New Testament picture was of a legitimate, autonomous, "secular" [21] power, charged with the task of maintaining social order, but not of spreading, maintaining or protecting the gospel of Jesus Christ.

The fact that such teaching was subverted over the centuries by those who came to see the Christian faith as *synonymous* with the social order, thereby legitimising coercion to maintain it, was a bad mistake - but a mistake, nonetheless.

The second exhibit for the defence relates to the fact that there are a plethora of counter-examples to be set against the theocratic ones outlined above. Western Christianity learnt the New Testament's lessons about state and Church the hard way. When Simon Blackburn writes, "the only reason Christians are not still burning each other is because the secular state stopped them," he is guilty of monumental historical illiteracy. The idea that the seventeenth century saw a brave cohort of secularists pull apart warring Christian factions, invent the concept of toleration and conjure the idea of "the secular state" from thin air is simply nonsense. Although the toleration in, say, 1700 was by no means unprecedented - Eastern Europe and, in particular, Poland-Lithuania was a beacon of tolerance in the sixteenth century - the simple fact is that it was Western Christians who discovered, from the exhaustion, demoralisation and carnage of a century of conflict, that theocracy was a singularly bad idea.

Such lessons took some time to sink in, of course, and no one seriously suggests that post-seventeenth century Christianity has been a three-hundred-year model of peace, tolerance and charity. The fact is, however, that those mainstream Christian denominations and movements established post-1700, from Methodism to Pentecostalism, have made no attempt to impose theocracy. Their public theologies have often varied widely but none has been theocratic in either theory or intent.

The same could be said of the nations founded by Christians post-1700, not least the most famous of them, the United States, which, to use Thomas Jefferson's famous phrase, deliberately erected "a wall of separation between Church and state".[22]

It is, therefore, paradoxical that the charge of Christian theocracy is levelled today against America more than any other nation on earth (with the obvious exceptions of Vatican City or Mount Athos) and so it is to America we must turn if we are to show that the theocratic sickness that plagued Christianity for much of its 2,000 year history is indeed cured.

the theocratic states of America?

Atheism is political suicide in America.

Until recently, not a single member of Congress had ever publicly admitted to being an atheist. Then, in March 2007, Congressman Pete Stark "came out" in response to a $1,000 bounty offered by the Secular Coalition for America for the "highest-level atheist, agnostic, humanist or any other kind of non-theist currently holding elected public office in the United States."[23]

> Atheism is political suicide in America.

According to a Gallup/USA Today poll of the previous month, Americans would rather vote for a presidential candidate who was Catholic, black, Jewish, female, Hispanic, Mormon, thrice-married, 72 years old, or homosexual than they would one who was an atheist.[24] Congressman Stark says he has no presidential ambitions.

God and Caesar mix a lot in America. At one end of the political spectrum, President George W Bush's ties with the "religious right" are well documented. Karl Rove, Bush's then chief political adviser, worked on the principle that the key to Republican victory in 2004 was the four million evangelical Christians who did not vote in 2000. Although the equation of Christianity, or even evangelicalism, with voting Republican is not quite as obvious as many think, there is no doubt that Christian "values voters" are critically important in any US election. Accordingly, throughout 2007 Republican presidential candidates paraded their Christian credentials in the recognition that failure to engage America's 140 million churchgoing Christians spelt certain defeat.

The popular perception that the Democrats are somehow antipathetic to Christian faith - "liberal", with all the many negative connotations that word has in US public discourse - has made their need to reach into America's Christian heartland even more urgent. Both leading candidates in the 2008 elections for the Democrat nomination employed full-time "faith outreach" officers and spoke openly and enthusiastically about their Christianity. Faith is a "crucial, though deeply personal, part of my life and my family's life," Hillary Clinton wrote in her 2003 autobiography, *Living History*.[25] "Religious commitment did not require me to suspend critical thinking," Barack Obama wrote in *Time* magazine in 2006. Nor did baptism make "the questions I had ... magically disappear. But, kneeling beneath that cross on the South Side of Chicago, I felt God's spirit beckoning me. I submitted myself to His will, and dedicated myself to discovering His truth."[26] Given all this eager God-talk among US politicians, is it surprising that people accuse America of being a theocracy?

And they do. Over recent years, a mini-publishing industry has emerged, exploring the US's alleged theocratic tendencies.[27] Arguments and explanations vary, but the general thrust is that the unprecedented influence that the "religious right" now enjoys is not simply politically unhealthy but constitutes a serious move towards state theocracy. Thus, Randall Balmer writes in *Thy Kingdom Come: An Evangelical's Lament*, "the Religious Right hankers for the kind of homogeneous theocracy that the Puritans tried to establish in seventeenth-century Massachusetts."[28]

The problem with such claims, however, is that whilst sounding plausible they are, on closer examination, rather difficult to justify. There are indeed some Christians in America who openly advocate theocracy. These "theonomists" (literally meaning people who follow God's law), known primarily as Christian Reconstructionists, take their cue from Rousas John Rushdoony whose massive *Institutes of Biblical Law* is "an exposition of the Decalogue as the blueprint for society".[29]

Although Rushdoony's writings have been popularised (using the word loosely) by several of his disciples, the fact is, as a writer in the American journal, *First Things*, acidly put it, Christian Reconstructionism "ranks somewhere between the Free Mumia movement and the Spartacist Youth League on the totem pole of political influence in America."[30] If you want credible evidence for American theocracy, you need to look elsewhere.

The most obvious place is not in what Christians say, but in what they do. You only have to look at the campaigns that the Christian Right have waged, to see their supposed theocratic agenda. They want, for example, to ban abortion, the teaching of evolution and same-sex partnerships. Further, they would like to put prayers back in school, and the Bible, in particular the Ten Commandments, in courthouses.

Putting aside the issue that none of these opinions is exactly a minority one in the US, the main problem with this line of argument is that for the most part, the "religious right" have been largely unsuccessful in their attempts. Abortion remains legal, evolution on the curriculum and civil partnerships an issue for state legislation. Prayer has no official role in school. The much publicised case of Roy's Rock, in which Alabama's chief justice lost his job in an attempt to keep a block of granite emblazoned with the Decalogue in the lobby of the state judicial building, simply underlines the continued strength of the First Amendment, separating Church and state. In the words of one commentator, "evangelicals signed a Faustian pact, handing over their mailing lists and votes in return for a conservative moral agenda. But those policies have gained them little."[31] One of the reasons (if only one) why the "religious right" gets so excited about "liberal America" is that, by and large, it is not getting its own way.

In any case, even were they to succeed, it is worth considering what the result would be. Ramesh Ponnuru, writing in the magazine *National Review*, put it this way:

> [The religious right] would generally prohibit abortion, and perhaps research that destroys human embryos. They would have the government refuse to accord legal standing to homosexual relationships. They would restrict pornography in various ways. They would have more prayer in schools, and less evolution. They think that religious groups should be able to participate in federal programs without compromising their beliefs. They would replace sex education with abstinence education. They want the government to promote marital stability … Nearly every one of these policies - and all of the most conservative ones - would merely turn the clock back to the late 1950s. That may be a very bad idea, but the America of the 1950s was not a theocracy.[32]

The reality is that, despite the best attempts to prove otherwise, the US neither is nor shows much sign of becoming a theocracy. What it is, however, is an overwhelmingly Christian population - and this is the "problem" that many accusations of theocracy cloak.

According to various polls, around 85% of Americans believe in God, 73% in miracles, 70% in "life after death", 70% in the existence of heaven, 70% that Jesus is the Son of God, 68% in angels, 66% in the resurrection, and roughly a third that the Bible is the actual word of God to be taken literally.[33] Two thirds claim they pray regularly and around half attend church each week.[34]

Not surprisingly, such beliefs and behaviour translate into attitudes towards the public square. Thus, 83% of Americans say that displays of Christmas symbols should be allowed on government property and 74% that it is proper to display the Ten Commandments in government buildings.[35] Furthermore, 69% of Americans claim that "liberals have gone too far in keeping religion out of schools and government", and 67% agree with the statement that the US is a Christian country.[36]

> The difference between the US, where politicians "don't do atheism" because it is political suicide, and the UK, where they "don't do God" because it is a political "disaster area", is not as great as we might think.

It is this culture, rather than America's alleged theocracy, that is the source of Congressman Pete Stark's problems. Because so many Americans are so self-consciously Christian, there is simply no point in American politicians "doing atheism".

This is something that should worry Christians just as much as it does secularists, but it is a problem inherent in all cultures that share a strongly-held common identity. The reason why John Stuart Mill wrote so passionately about the need to defend the "contrary opinion" of "only one person" from everyone else was because he recognised that majorities are naturally tyrannous.[37]

We in Britain may bemoan this uncomfortably homogeneous state of affairs, but it is worth noting that the difference between the US, where politicians "don't do atheism" because it is political suicide, and the UK, where they "don't do God" because it is a political "disaster area", is not as great as we might think.[38]

The reality is that accusations of American theocracy, and the attendant calls for Christians to back out of politics, are motivated either by a dislike of the US' prevailing Christian culture or, more specifically, by a dislike of what the largest and loudest element of that Christian culture favours. This point was well made by Russ Douthat in the journal *First Things*:

> After years of blasting any religious encroachment on the political sphere as a threat to the Constitution, the *New York Times* editorial page awoke to find Cardinal Roger Mahony advocating civil disobedience by Catholics to protest an immigration bill - and immediately praised the cardinal for adding "a moral dimension to what has largely been a debate about politics and economics".[39]

The fact that the US is a comparatively homogeneous Christian culture rather than a theocracy should not, in itself, become a cause for complacency. Religious majorities can be as tyrannous as any other, which is why attempts to dismantle the First Amendment need resisting, even if they have widespread support, although there is little sign that they do. Similarly, there are many attitudes and stances associated with the "religious right" - its largely unquestioning support for the "war on terror", its willingness to marry Christianity with nationalist sentiment, its bad eschatology, its naïve association with the Republican party,[40] its troubling views on evolutionary theory and, at least until recently, climate change - that need to be challenged.

However, none amounts to evidence that American Christianity is theocratic in theory or intent, and none constitutes a justification for confining Christian opinions to the private realm. As John Witte Jr. has written, the "religious right's" recent rise to prominence in the public square and in the political process:

> should not be met with glib talk of censorship or reflexive incantation of Jefferson's mythical wall of separation. [Rather it] should be met with the equally strong rise of the Christian left, of the Christian middle, and of sundry Jewish, Muslim, Hindu, Buddhist, and other groups who test and contest its premises and policies. That is how a healthy democracy works.[41]

conclusion

If we have dwelt at some length on the issue of theocracy, it is because it is a serious one. Secular criticisms of mixing religion and politics often resort to bombast and caricature, but the best are serious and demand respect. Given Christianity's constant temptation to dominate the political process for its own ends over the last 2,000 years, those who advocate a strong Christian engagement in the public square in modern Britain need to be able to counter the argument that if you give Christians an inch, they will take the entire political playing field.

This chapter has argued that whilst Christianity has tended towards theocracy of one type or another on many occasions over its history, there is little reason to fear that it will do so again in twenty-first century Britain. Western Christianity, in particular, has learnt its public theology through experience. The New Testament is clear about the legitimacy of an autonomous political arena, which is not there to do the Church's job so much as to protect the social order. By 1700, Christianity was beginning to get the message. Modern America, the example so often cited to prove that this theocratic temptation is alive and kicking, in fact does nothing of the kind. Those who make the accusation tend to do so because it is easier than actually arguing with their numerous, well-entrenched and recently ascendant opponents.

Theology and history thus offer two credible exhibits for the defence against the accusation of theocracy. It is the third, however, that is most persuasive. Simply put, there is not a single Christian leader or mainstream thinker anywhere in the UK who is advocating anything even approaching theocracy. What they are advocating is the subject of the next chapter.

chapter 1 - references

1   For Madagascar see http://news.bbc.co.uk/1/hi/world/africa/6763947.stm
2   Philip Pullman, "The war on words," the *Guardian*, 6 November 2004:
    http://books.guardian.co.uk/review/story/0,,1343733,00.html
3   Jackie Ashley, "Cardinals, back off from this war with women and state," the *Guardian*, 4 June 2007:
    http://www.guardian.co.uk/commentisfree/story/0,,2094774,00.html. For a response to Jackie Ashley
    see, Jonathan Chaplin, "Can secularism learn to love pluralism?" www.theosthinktank.co.uk
4   AC Grayling, "Religions don't deserve special treatment," the *Guardian*, 19 October 2006:
    http://commentisfree.guardian.co.uk/ac_grayling/2006/10/acgrayling.html. See also his "Keep God
    out of public affairs", the *Observer*, 12 August 2001:
    http://observer.guardian.co.uk/comment/story/0,,535543,00.html
5   Simon Blackburn, "Against the grain: Religion should be kept out of politics," the *Independent*, 5 April
    2007: http://education.independent.co.uk/higher/article2420566.ece
6   Karen Armstrong, *The Battle for God: Fundamentalism in Judaism, Christianity and Islam*
    (HarperCollins, 2003)
7   See Spencer, *Doing God*, pp. 21-30, for a fuller engagement with this question
8   Josephus Flavius, *Contra Apion*, II.17
9   Philip Pullman, "The war on words"
10 Nigel G Wright, "Participating without Possessing: The public and the private in Christian
    Discipleship," Lecture delivered to the 125th anniversary gathering of the Industrial Chaplains'
    Fellowship at St Ethelburga's Church, City of London on 26 November 2003
11 Oliver O'Donovan and Joan Lockwood O'Donovan, *From Irenaeus to Grotius: A Sourcebook in Christian
    Political Thought* (Cambridge: Eerdmans, 1999), p. 132
12 St Augustine, *The Correction of the Donatists*, chapter 23
13 An even better example of theocracy may be seen in Umayyad caliphate, which was influenced by
    Orthodoxy, during the first Islamic century. According to Hans Kung, "the Christian-Byzantine model
    of the 'symphony' of throne and altar differentiated Church and state, for all their unity, whereas the
    first Arab empire, that of the Umayyads, which took over the Byzantine administrative apparatus with
    many of its organisational structures, remained a theocracy in keeping with its origins - its head was
    the caliph as God's representative. He had not only political but also religious authority." See Hans
    Kung, *Islam: Past, Present and Future* (OneWorld, 2007), p. 586. Perhaps the purest example of
    theocracy is when the political authority in question does not simply represent God, but is deemed to
    be God. See the book of Judith, chapter 6, in which the Ammonite leader Achior is asked by
    Holofernes, general-in-chief of the Assyrian army, "And who is God if not Nebuchadnezzar?" (verse 2)
14 I am grateful to Jonathan Chaplin for these points, correcting my initial (mis)understanding of Calvin's
    Geneva as a hierocracy
15 Diarmaid MacCulloch, *Reformation: Europe's House Divided 1490-1700* (Allen Lane, 2003), pp. 237-53.
    See also Philip Benedict, *Christ's Churches Purely Reformed: A Social History of Calvinism* (Yale
    University Press, 2002)
16 MacCulloch comments that "if one would have been justified in anticipating a good night out in the
    company of Martin Luther, the same cannot be said of the buttoned-up French exile who wanted to
    stop the citizens of Geneva dancing"
17 See Spencer, *Doing God*, chapter 2 for more details on this
18 O'Donovan and O'Donovan, *Irenaeus*, p. 131
19 Christopher Wright, *Old Testament Ethics for the People of God* (IVP, 2004), pp. 392-99
20 The term "state" is, of course, rather anachronistic in this context but will have to suffice
21 "Secular" here refers to the concept of a political arena belonging to "this age", "a public space in
    which authorities should be respected but could legitimately be challenged and could never accord
    to themselves absolute or ultimate significance," rather than the non- or anti-religious meaning it
    often has today. See Spencer, *Doing God*, pp. 37-38

22 Letter to Danbury Baptist Association, 1 January 1802. It should be noted that some early colonies, like Massachusetts, still held to the territorial principle with regard to religion (see below)
23 Matt Wells, "Must the US president believe in God?" BBC On-line, 20 July 2007: http://news.bbc.co.uk/1/hi/world/americas/6906693.stm; "Could Christian vote desert Republicans?" 27 July 2007: http://news.bbc.co.uk/1/hi/world/americas/6917947.stm; Alex Massie, "US congressman breaks the last big taboo," Scotsman.com, 15 March 2007; http://news.scotsman.com/topics.cfm?tid=1359&id=404482007
24 Jeffrey M Jones, "Some Americans Reluctant to Vote for Mormon, 72-Year-Old Presidential Candidates," Gallup Poll, 20 February 2007: http://www.galluppoll.com/content/?ci=26611&pg=1
25 Hillary Clinton, *Living History*, (Simon & Schuster, 2003)
26 Barack Obama, "My spiritual journey," *Time* magazine, October 2006: http://www.time.com/time/magazine/article/0,9171,1546579-6,00.html
27 See, for example, Randall Balmer, *Thy Kingdom Come: How The Religious Right Distorts the Faith and Threatens America: An Evangelical's Lament* (Basic Books, 2006); Kevin Phillips, *American Theocracy: The Peril and Politics of Radical Religion, Oil, and Borrowed Money in the 21st Century* (Viking, 2006); James Rudin, *The Baptizing of America: The Religious Right's Plans for the Rest of Us* (Thunder's Mouth, 2005); Chris Hedges, *American Fascists: The Christian Right and the War On America* (Free Press, 2007); Michelle Goldberg, *Kingdom Coming: The Rise of Christian Nationalism* (WW Norton, 2006)
28 Balmer, *Thy Kingdom Come*, p.181
29 Wright, *Old Testament Ethics*, pp. 403-408
30 Ross Douthat, "Theocracy Theocracy Theocracy," First Things, August/September 2006
31 Tim Watkin, "Religious Right Turn," the *Guardian*, 12 February 2008
32 Quoted in Douthat, "Theocracy"
33 Jennifer Harper, "Majority in US Believes in God," *Washington Times*, December 2005: http://pewforum.org/news/display.php?NewsID=5981. See also Gallup News: http://www.galluppoll.com/content/?ci=27877&pg=1; and The Pew Forum on Religion and Public Life: http://pewforum.org/news/display.php?NewsID=4247
34 BBC, "What the world thinks of God": http://news.bbc.co.uk/1/shared/spl/hi/programmes/wtwtgod/pdf/wtwtogod.pdf
35 The Pew Forum on Religion and Public Life, "Religious Displays and the Courts," June 2007: http://pewforum.org/docs/?DocID=232
36 The Pew Forum on Religion and Public Life, "Many Americans uneasy with mix of religion and politics," August 2006: http://pewforum.org/docs/?DocID=153
37 John Stuart Mill, *On Liberty* (1859)
38 Alistair Campbell, *The Blair Years* (Hutchinson 2007), entry for Monday, 8 April 1996
39 Douthat, "Theocracy"
40 "When preachers echo GOP talking points rather than shape them, they risk going down the same path trod by the liberal clerics of the 1960s, whose sermons became indistinguishable from the gospel according to the *New York Times* - until, as David Frum once put it, their parishioners began to wonder 'why they should spend a Sunday morning listening to the same editorial twice?'" Ross Douthat, "Theocracy"
41 John Witte Jr., "Should there be a 'wall of separation' between Church and State?", www.theosthinktank.co.uk

what Christians advocate

The debate about what role Christianity should play in the public square often gets stuck in a sterile "either/or". Either it, indeed all religious faith, is privatised or we will end up living in a theocracy. Either Christian principles are explicitly recognised as the foundation of British public life or that life will become irreparably relativised and individualistic.

The reality is, of course, more complex, with Christianity having played a variety of different roles vis-à-vis public life through its history. Perhaps the most famous categorisation of these was made by the twentieth century American theologian and ethicist, H Richard Niebuhr. In his book *Christ and Culture* Niebuhr outlined five ways in which Christianity had related to the cultures in which it had found itself through history. These were "Christ against Culture", in which Christianity is set against, critiques and often retreats from the culture in which it finds itself; "Christ of Culture", in which the sacred within culture is discovered and that which is most Christ-like is celebrated; "Christ and Culture in Paradox", in which the relationship between the two is dialectical, rather than simply oppositional or accommodating; "Christ above Culture", in which Christianity provides the context for, affirms but also judges its host culture; and "Christ the Transformer of Culture", in which Christ "redeems and transforms" public culture.[1]

Niebuhr's categorisation is not the only one. The German theologian Ernst Troeltsch, writing half a century before Niebuhr, saw three rather than five models of engagement: "church-type", characterised by an outward-looking engagement with the world; "sect-type", characterised by a more inward-looking withdrawal from public engagement; and "mysticism", which remained "entirely in the realm of private spiritual experience".[2]

Such categorisations are useful in showing how our all-or-nothing picture today is misleading and unhelpful. They can, however, feel somewhat arbitrary and, as such, not especially helpful as a means of understanding the current British situation, in particular the stances taken by Christian leaders and denominations regarding the appropriate public role of the Christian faith.

Rather than draw directly on them, this chapter will explore how the earliest Church engaged in the public square and then use the resulting model as a means of understanding current UK positions.

the earliest Church

Jesus' first disciples enjoyed a brief period, following his resurrection and ascension, in which they lived and worshipped in Jerusalem without significant interference. This was hardly a honeymoon period. St Luke is clear in his Acts of the Apostles that the authorities disliked, antagonised and, on occasion, arrested members of the new sect. However, compared to the full-scale persecution that followed the execution of Stephen, it was a period of relative stability.

Examining this earliest period of the Church's life is unlikely to provide us with a blueprint for its public life today. Quite apart from anything else, the first Christians were more interested in working out what the new life of the Kingdom of God meant for their community than they were in articulating precisely how that community should engage with wider public life.

Nevertheless, Scripture does offer guidelines in this area, which can be adapted as a framework for our contemporary situation. Chapters 1 to 5 of Luke's Acts of the Apostles focus primarily on the activity of a very small number of leading disciples, primarily Peter and John. Their stories, combined with three shorter, interspersed accounts of the wider Church,[3] reveal a four-fold pattern of engagement in the public square, based on public proclamation, public assembly, public action and public confrontation. We shall briefly examine each of these in turn.

public proclamation

One of our fundamental errors today is to see Christianity as a belief to be held or an experience to be felt. Whilst it undoubtedly involves both these factors, it is first and foremost a story to be told. That story acts as an invitation to, among other things, certain beliefs and experiences, but it remains, primarily, a story to be told, in public, about what God has done, is doing and will do.

This public proclamation is clear from Jesus' first public words, "Repent and believe the good news," (Mark 1.15) as it is also clear from those of his disciples in Acts. Following the events of Pentecost, Luke tells us that, "Peter stood up with the Eleven, raised his voice and addressed the crowd." (Acts 2.14) The motif is repeated in subsequent chapters.

> *Christianity is first and foremost a story to be told.*

When Peter attracts an "astonished" crowd after healing a crippled beggar on the Temple steps, he turns to address them. (Acts 3.11) In a brief summary of the early Church's life, at the end of Acts chapter 4, Luke tells us, "with great power the apostles continued to testify to the resurrection of the Lord Jesus." (Acts 4.33) Similarly, when the apostles are arrested in the following chapter, it was to prevent them publicly teaching the crowds about Jesus: "We gave you strict orders not to teach in this name." (Acts 5.28)

Public proclamation was, and is, the *sine qua non* of the Church's public life. The gospel, as Bishop Lesslie Newbigin once wrote, is "public truth".[4]

public assembly

The opening chapters of Acts maintain a close focus on a small number of Jesus' first followers, with the wider picture of the early Church only discernible at the margins.

On three occasions, however, Luke consciously stands back and offers us a brief sketch of the early Church. These brief glimpses provide us with a second element of the early Church's public life, one that we, in the free West, are inclined to overlook: public assembly.

It is clear that Jesus' first followers met together in private. Luke tells us that when "they returned to Jerusalem from … the Mount of Olives [following the ascension] … they went upstairs to the room where they were staying … [and] they all joined together constantly in prayer." (Acts 1.12-14)

> *The early Church lived not simply as a community, but as an intentionally publicly visible community.*

He is also clear, however, that they met regularly in public. In his first summary of the early Church's life, Luke tells us that "every day they continued to meet together in the temple courts," going on to say, "they [also] broke bread in their homes and ate together." (Acts 2.46)

Similarly, in his second summary, he records that "all the believers used to meet together in Solomon's Colonnade," before adding, "no one else dared join them, even though they were highly regarded by the people." (Acts 5.12-13)

In this way, the early Church lived not simply as a community, but as an intentionally *publicly visible* community.

public action

Gangs hang out together. Mere public assembly does not, in itself, merit respect, let alone the esteem in which Luke claimed the Church was held.

Luke's three summaries of the early Church's life provide a clue to the source of that esteem. Simply put, it was that the Church did not just gather in the public square but acted corporately and charitably there.

Luke informs us, in chapter 2 verse 45, that "selling their possessions and goods, [the apostles] gave to anyone as he had need."

His later summary, in chapter 4, elucidates this picture of public generosity:

> There were no needy persons among them. For from time to time those who
> owned lands or houses sold them, brought the money from the sales and put
> it at the apostles' feet, and it was distributed to anyone as he had need. Crowds
> gathered also from the towns around Jerusalem, bringing their sick and those
> tormented by evil spirits, and all of them were healed.
>
> [Acts 4.34-36]

Finally, in chapter 5, Luke tells us, "the apostles performed many miraculous signs
and wonders among the people." (Acts 5.12)

Between them, these three vignettes give us an idea of the early Church's public
action, in which the nascent community helped and healed those within and
beyond its immediate boundaries in an expression of God's own action in Christ.

public confrontation

Public confrontation is readily (mis)understood as a form of would-be violent
insurrection, the action of a group that is not getting its way and is prepared to
bypass the conventional channels of consultation in pursuing its objectives.

Whilst undoubtedly accurate for some instances, this model is singularly unhelpful
in understanding the pattern of the early Church, which, as we noted in the
previous chapter, seems to have been largely respectful in its attitude to the public
authorities.

The respect that Paul requires of the early Church was not, however, a kind of
supine timidity, an unquestioning "Yes" to anything demanded by the powers that
be - as his own life illustrates. The picture we have in the early chapters of Acts is
of a Church willing to stand for what it feels it must in order to be itself. If that
involved confrontation with the authorities, so be it. This was not insurrection or
revolution so much as a public commitment to an alternative authority, an
alternative narrative, alternative values and loyalties, a commitment that could
cause tension with the contemporary public authorities.

Thus, when Peter and John were told by the Sanhedrin that they may "no longer
... speak or teach at all in the name of Jesus," they replied, "judge for yourselves
whether it is right in God's sight to obey you rather than God ... we cannot help
speaking about what we have seen and heard." (Acts 4.17-19)

The exchange is repeated on their next appearance before the Sanhedrin. The
High Priest again accuses the apostles of ignoring the "strict orders not to teach in

this name", and instead, of having "filled Jerusalem with your teaching". Peter and the other apostles replied, "we must obey God rather than men! ... We are witnesses of these things [relating to Jesus]." (Acts 5.29-32)

This is not armed rebellion but rather a stubborn insistence that being a Christian demands certain things - in this instance public proclamation, although the confrontation in Acts 4 is ostensibly "for an act of kindness [i.e. healing] shown to a cripple". No matter how much the authorities will it otherwise, this is not open for debate.

The Church's public confrontation is thus not aggressive so much as determined. It is the maintenance of certain beliefs and practices against the pressure to change them, rather than an active rebelling against the authorities. The apostles' words are a foretaste of Martin Luther's more famous (although probably apocryphal), "Here I stand. I can do no other. God help me."

Acts 1 to 5 is only a brief sketch of the earliest moments of the early Church and it would be foolhardy to take from it a blueprint for the Church's public action at all times and in all places. However, it is worth noting that this four-fold picture of public proclamation, public assembly, public action and public confrontation is evident elsewhere in the New Testament, where we see certain individuals dedicating their lives and risking public confrontation in order to proclaim the gospel and nurture communities in which people would "live such good lives ... that, though [pagans] accuse you of doing wrong, they may see your good deeds and glorify God." (1 Peter 2.12)

It is also telling that this four-fold picture provides a good framework for understanding current positions on the public role of the Church in modern Britain. We shall examine three such positions relating to three of the largest Christian constituencies in the UK below, starting with Anglicanism, through the thought of the Head of the Anglican Communion, Rowan Williams.

Rowan Williams

Rowan Williams is widely recognised and respected, by Christians and non-Christians alike, as one of the country's leading public intellectuals. Although his position as Archbishop of Canterbury and Head of the Anglican Communion does not permit him to inform the Church's teaching with the same authority as the Pope with the Catholic Church, his speeches have a significant weight (in more than one sense of the word), and any analysis of Anglicanism's current attitude to the proper public role of Christianity must attend to his views.

Since becoming Archbishop of Canterbury in 2002, Williams has spoken on the public role of Christianity on a number of occasions.[5] Although coming at the topic from a number of angles, many of his talks take time to emphasise the point that Christianity has no right or remit to force its creeds or ethics upon the population through political means:

> The Christian vision is not … one in which the person's choice is overridden by a religiously-backed public authority.[6]

> Wilberforce and his circle … were deeply preoccupied with personal morality; but they did not seek to enforce purely personal morality by public legislation.[7]

Williams' repeated emphasis of this point reflects, in part, an awareness of popular suspicions about mixing religion and politics. But it also marks an honesty and alertness to the kind of theocratic temptations discussed in the previous chapter. "Christianity has a mixed history of relation with political power," he told an audience in St Andrew's Cathedral in Singapore. "When churches have directly tried to exercise political power, they have often compromised their real character as communities of free mutual giving and service."[8]

> *The Christian vision is not one in which the person's choice is overridden by a religiously-backed public authority.*

"[The] Enlightenment assumption [of rational and universal grounds for ethics] is powerful and attractive partly because of a collective memory of centuries of appeal to unaccountable and tyrannical religious authority," he said in a lecture on church schools.[9] And more bluntly still, at an address at the European Policy Centre, Brussels:

> In practice, of course, the Church has most often been an enemy to what we should instinctively see as democratising or liberalising moves in a nation's history.[10]

This intense disquiet about the direct linking of Christian faith and political power does not, of course, constitute a call for withdrawal from the public square. Rather it is a call to engage in public life in the way that is truest to Christianity itself.

While no single lecture describes comprehensively and in detail what this should be, Williams' various talks outline a vision that corresponds well with the four-fold framework outlined above. First, there is the task of public proclamation. Responding to the announcement that he was to become the 104th Archbishop of Canterbury, Williams described how his "primary job" was "to go on being a priest and a bishop … to celebrate God and what God has done in Jesus".[11] His principal task within this was "that of any ordained teacher … to point to the source without which none of our activity would make sense - the gift of God as it is set before us in the Bible and Christian belief."

Of all the four elements outlined above, however, public proclamation is also the most elusive within Williams' thinking. This is due, in part, to his often elliptical style, but also to the *assumption* that this is what Christians should do, with the more difficult and interesting question being, "*how* should they do it?" Williams is acutely aware of the problems of "speak[ing] of God … in the middle of a culture which, while it may show a great deal of nostalgia, fascination and even hunger for the spiritual, is generally sceptical of Christianity and the Church."

Thus, his focus has been less on telling "the old, old story", and more on spelling out what it means for our new, new world. "If there is one thing I long for above all else," he said at the conclusion to his response to being elevated to Canterbury, "[it] is that the years to come will see Christianity in this country able to capture the imagination of our culture." It is this ambition, as much as any other, that has inspired Williams' wide range of lectures on topics such as the media, prison reform, education, Europe, trust and the democratic process. In spite of superficial appearances, public proclamation of the gospel lies at the heart of most of Williams' speeches.

Second is the business of public assembly. In a nation in which the right of assembly is so well-established, this may seem a rather incidental point. But, as noted above, this is not simply a call for the Church to be a kind of ecclesiastical gang that hangs out on street corners. Rather, it is linked to the tasks of public proclamation and public action. It means being a "visible", "alternative" community:

> The Church of Christ begins by defining itself as a community both alongside political society and of a different order to political society.[12]

> Churches do not campaign for political control … but for public visibility - for the capacity to argue for and defend their vision in the public sphere.[13]

> [Their] main task is to create "spaces" for an alternative story - to challenge the self-evidence of the narrative of secular modernity.[14]

This public assembly is closely linked with the task of public action, life and work that humanises us:

> The religious community needs to be clear about its primary responsibility as a place where people are formed in moral vision by shared practice.[15]

> Christian involvement in the public sphere is visible celebration of the sacramental reality by which believers live, and the devising and implementing of usually small-scale projects suggesting possibilities for human beings different from those assumed by contractual and acquisitive stories.[16]

All this may sound rather comfortable, and even acquiescent, but Williams is clear, in his own academic and understated way, that this kind of public proclamation, assembly and action is liable to present a challenge to the rest of society:

> Christians are called, it seems, to live out the vision of relationships in the Body of Christ without fear of conflict with the rest of society; because sometimes that living out of these relationships can be unpopular with society.[17]

The confrontation is not, at least in the first instance, a narrowly political challenge to the status quo. Rather the Church will be a challenge to society just by being itself:

> The Church as a political agent has to be a community capable of telling its own story and its own stories, visible as a social body and thus making claims upon human loyalty. While not a simple rival to the secular state, it will inevitably raise questions about how the secular state thinks of loyalty and indeed of social unity or cohesion.[18]

> [The Church is] a voice that questions from a wholly different perspective ... a conversation partner ... a critical friend to the state and its laws. It asks about the foundations of what the state takes for granted and often challenges the shallowness of a prevailing social morality. It pushes for change to make the state a little more like the community that it is itself representing, the Kingdom of God.[19]

Accordingly, Williams noted in a lecture given at the Pontifical Academy of Social Sciences that genuine political freedom:

> needs to be the freedom to ask some fundamental questions about the climate and direction of a society as shown in its policy decisions.[20]

This is not to say that confrontation is necessarily political. It might just as well be social, as the nineteenth century campaign for the reform of "Public Manners" showed:

> [Wilberforce's] campaign ... with which the Clapham group was so closely associated was about confronting the ethos and assumptions of a culture, but not about imposing morality by statute.[21]

In case it needs stating, none of this constitutes a licence for social rebellion:

> For the sake of common public order, the legality of what the state decides is normally (if not invariably) to be accepted, even if its morality is still challenged.[22]

Confrontation, if it comes about, is most likely to take the form of "the much misunderstood tradition in Anglican thinking of ... 'passive obedience'":

If government enacts what the conscientious believer cannot accept, the believer obeys "passively", accepting that if he or she breaks the law they will legally and legitimately suffer the consequences, but still refusing to act in any way that could support the general enforcing of a specific law that is problematic. It is the claim to a space for conscientious dissent that may question but does not try to negate the effect of a particular law. That is to say, it allows room for peaceful civil disobedience, while accepting the legal consequences of this; it does not sanction violent or anti-constitutional resistance.[23]

As the experience of Peter, John and the early apostles indicated, however, the nature and extent of this confrontation will depend, not so much on the Church as on the ethos of the state:

If the state enacts or perpetuates in the corporate life of the nation what is directly contrary to the Christian understanding of God's purpose for humanity - if it endorses slavery, for example - the Christian is bound to protest and to argue in the public sphere for change, through whatever channels are available.[24]

Overall, the four-fold framework of public proclamation, public assembly, public action and public confrontation works well as a means of understanding Rowan Williams' agenda for Christian engagement in the public square today. That engagement should not "deliver us either into theocracy or into an entirely naked public space", but rather take the form of "witness [to] ... the values of the Kingdom of God in ordinary life."[25]

Free Churches

The Free (or Dissenting or Nonconformist) Church tradition in Britain is as old as the Anglican one, dating back to the mid-sixteenth century. Originally comprising a relatively limited number of groups, today it covers a huge range, including the Baptist Union, Methodist Church, United Reformed Church and Salvation Army, alongside newer, independent Church groups, such as Assemblies of God, New Frontiers and Vineyard.

The number of Free Church denominations and the way in which many are organised prevents there being any authoritative, universally applicable Free Church statement on the role of Christianity in modern Britain. Indeed, some Churches, because they are "bound together in covenant rather than by structures that exercise authority over the whole," are deeply uneasy about issuing definitive statements at all.[26] Consequently, any statement on the Free Church's attitude to Christian engagement in the public square is bound to be an oversimplification and vulnerable to counter-examples.

That recognised, a number of the larger denominations have issued statements on this subject, and many Free Churches belong to umbrella organisations, like the Free Churches' Group or Evangelical Alliance (EA), which have explored the question themselves.[27] Accordingly, this section draws on several denominational statements, as well as two particular EA publications - *Faith and Nation* and *Movement for Change* - which reflect that organisation's interest in public theology.[28]

Not surprisingly, the Free Churches are acutely aware of the diversity of opinion that exists within the Christian community. The structure of some Churches, like the Baptist, preclude authoritative statements on the appropriate nature of Christian public engagement and even those Free Churches with a more centralised structure acknowledge a range of legitimate opinions:

> In putting our vision into practice, Christians reveal further divisions among themselves. These divisions have remained unresolved over many generations. For example, many hold that participation in political life is the prerogative of individual Christians; while others insist that the Christian community, as a body and an institution, is called to a corporate witness in the political and social realm.[29]

Despite this, however, the four-fold framework outlined above describes the Free Church "position" reasonably well. The business of public proclamation of the gospel is paramount. The first of the United Reformed Church's "Five Marks of Mission" is to "proclaim the good news of the Kingdom". William Booth, who founded the Salvation Army, earned his reputation not primarily as a social activist but as a uniquely powerful preacher. The Evangelical Alliance remarks in its *Faith and Nation* report:

> One of the most fundamental freedoms for Christians is liberty to proclaim the gospel ... as Evangelical Christians, we ... must go on believing that Christ is the Saviour ... and ... go on asserting our right to proclaim Him freely as such in the public arena.[30]

Public proclamation does not, however, simply mean shouting the gospel at anybody, irrespective of whether they are listening, a point EA publications emphasise, perhaps because aware that evangelicals sometimes do just that:

> Movement from being heard primarily to convey a message of condemnation to proclaiming the language of compassion is an imperative for people claiming to advance the Kingdom of God in the current context.[31]

Similarly, the Baptist Union of Great Britain remarks that whilst:

> the [Baptist] church always needs to be careful about when it chooses to have a voice, not least to ensure that it has something meaningful to say into a

situation … it can be argued that it is our Christian responsibility to speak [on public issues].

Public proclamation is thus, again, not only telling the story but also articulating its implication in a measured and "meaningful" way.

The New Testament documents seem to suggest that the best mechanism for delivering social transformation would be the Christian community living as Jesus intended.

Alongside the task of proclaiming the gospel publicly runs the practice of public assembly. As one would expect from Churches with a more congregational and less hierarchical structure, the business of assembly is of utmost significance. "Baptists believe that the Church of Christ finds clear expression within the life of a local congregation."[32]

Once again, however, this is not simply gathering together in order to socialise, nor even for mutual edification. Rather, Christians should come together as "a partnership-based community, a koinonia [fellowship], shaped by a manifesto originating in love."[33] It is by doing this in public that the Church "will portray a righteousness, justice, liberty and wholeness that cannot help but be noticed by the wider community."[34] This practice is rooted strongly in that of the New Testament Church:

> Rather than insisting their ethics be adapted by society in general, the [first Christian] believers concentrated on making disciples who would adopt the Christian ethic … the New Testament documents seem to suggest that the best mechanism for delivering social transformation would be the Christian community living as Jesus intended.[35]

And it is this practice that has reappeared time and again throughout the history of the Church. For example:

> In an environment devoid of any other institutional fabric for local civil society, the [early Methodist] chapel would quickly become a focus of the community, providing education, mutual support, social interaction and leisure interest as well as spiritual and moral instruction … There is a revealing parallel to be drawn here with the upsurge of Pentecostalism in Latin America since the 1960s, where amidst a similar process of rapid economic and social change new evangelical churches have become an important focus for the building of local community.[36]

This last quotation illustrates the now familiar link between public assembly and public action. Linked as they are, however, it is important not to blur their distinctions. The Church will become "a focus of the community, providing education, mutual support, [and] social interaction," not when Christians come together with that objective in mind, but when they come together for the primary purpose of communion, with God and each other. Only when this order is preserved - assembly (public or otherwise) that leads to action - will that action be effective. The EA quotes the US Mennonite theologian John Howard Yoder:

> The church must be a sample of the kind of humanity within which, for example, economic and racial differences are surmounted. Only then will it have anything to say to the society that surrounds it about how those differences must be dealt with.[37]

This is not to belittle the need for public action, but rather to see public action take its place as the fruit rather than the cause of public assembly. The fact that, for example, the United Reformed Church places its mission to "respond to human need by loving service" *after* that of "proclaim[ing] the good news of the Kingdom" is testimony to how this order it preserved by Free Churches, as is the fact that the Salvation Army introduces its very extensive list of public action by saying, "we demonstrate our Christian principles through social welfare provision."

Finally, the Free Churches are no less aware than Rowan Williams of the potential for confrontation between the state and the Church. The Methodist Church has said:

> The Christian community becomes involved in the exercise of political responsibility and supports in prayer those who exercise political authority, as it prays for all people according to their need. However, walking in the way of the cross means that faithfulness to the Christian vision will frequently provoke conflict with political powers; and that Christians will bring to all political and social issues a keen critical perspective.[38]

Similarly, the United Reformed Church remarks that:

> Jesus often confronted those with political, economic and social power, challenging them to consider the values upon which they operated. Our calling to follow him today places a similar responsibility on us. The Church's "Five Marks of Mission" reflect this when they call us to … seek to transform unjust structures of society.[39]

One of the most notable reports of recent years, the EA's *Faith and Nation*, contained a long discussion on the subject of "Christians and Civil Disobedience". This was reported in the *Sunday Telegraph* as "a leading church group … rais[ing] the prospect of civil unrest and even 'violent revolution' to protect religious freedoms," a summary that does the analysis little justice.[40] The report actually says:

If, as most Christians accept, they should be politically involved in democratic processes, many believe this may, where necessary, take the form of active resistance to the state. This can take different forms and may encompass disobedience to law, civil disobedience, involving selective, non-violent resistance or protest, or ultimately violent revolution.[41]

The reference to "violent revolution" may have been ill-advised, as was a subsequent reference to "deliberate defiance and even perhaps revolution" in the same discussion, but the report is also clear that:

there are very few matters where state action may be unambiguously recognised by Christians as perpetrating evil that has to be resisted by deliberate acts of defiance, [and that] Christians must take great care not to provoke unnecessary confrontation.[42]

As with Rowan Williams and the earliest Church, confrontation with the public authorities is not something that the Free Churches seek or welcome. But it is something they recognise as a possibility.

Roman Catholicism

Our final example of contemporary Christian attitudes to the public role of Christianity in modern Britain comes from the largest denomination, with perhaps the most clearly ordered social doctrine, Roman Catholicism.

Here, the recently published *Compendium of the Social Doctrine of the Church* is invaluable, drawing, as it does, on over a century of encyclical letters, Church councils and other documents. To this can be added Pope Benedict XVI's papal encyclicals *Deus Caritas Est* and *Spe Salvi*, various pronouncements from the Catholic Bishops' Conference of England and Wales, such as *The Common Good and the Catholic Church's Social Teaching*, and a number of speeches made by Cardinal Cormac Murphy-O'Connor.[43]

From this variety of sources emerges a vision of the Church's public life that fits well with the four-fold pattern of Acts 1 to 5.

First, as with Rowan Williams' writings, there is an acknowledgement of Christianity's theocratic temptation. This point is repeated in various Church documents. The Second Vatican Council solemnly reaffirmed that, "in their proper spheres, the political community and the Church are mutually independent and self-governing,"[44] and John Paul II wrote in *Centesimus Annus*:

Since it is not an ideology, the Christian faith does not presume to imprison changing socio-political realities in a rigid schema ... The Church respects the legitimate autonomy of the democratic order...[45]

More explicitly still, his successor, Benedict XVI, wrote in his first encyclical *Deus Caritas Est*:

> Catholic social doctrine … has no intention of giving the Church power over the State. Even less is it an attempt to impose on those who do not share the faith ways of thinking and modes of conduct proper to faith … The Church cannot and must not take upon herself the political battle to bring about the most just society possible. She cannot and must not replace the State. [46]

> *The Church cannot and must not take upon herself the political battle to bring about the most just society possible. She cannot and must not replace the State.*

Rather, the Church's primary public function "is to fulfil the purpose for which the Holy Spirit was poured out on [her] - to proclaim Jesus Christ." [47] In the words of *Centesimus Annus*:

> The Church renders [her] service to human society by preaching the truth about the creation of the world, which God has placed in human hands so that people may make it fruitful and more perfect through their work; and by preaching the truth about the Redemption, whereby the Son of God has saved mankind and at the same time has united all people, making them responsible for one another. [48]

Such sentiments were echoed by Cardinal Cormac Murphy-O'Connor in a lecture on the role of the Church in contemporary Europe:

> One of the main tasks of the Church must be … to act as the repository of the continent's tradition, not by resorting to simplistic answers or a stance of opposition and rejection, but by recalling Europe to its roots in God, the God who in his dying and rising for us showed us the dignity of the human person and the transcendent meaning of human relationships. [49]

As we will readily recognise now, this does not just mean talk. In the words of the *Compendium of Social Doctrine of the Church*:

> the Church's social doctrine has the task of proclamation … [but] this is done not only on the level of principles but also in practice. [50]

This practice is first and foremost that of nurturing a community that is seen to be different:

> From earliest times, the centrality of the community has been part of the essential shape of the Church. The Church must be seen to be creatively building community by valuing the resources and gifts of all, and especially … those of the ones most despised by society. [51]

> The Church cannot neglect the service of charity any more than she can neglect the Sacraments and the Word.

It is only when this "creatively [built] community" is in place, that the Church's public action will stand any chance of transforming society:

> When the Church lives, in the core of its being, the Trinitarian value of communion, it provides the energy and the inspiration for the creation of authentic communities in our society.[52]

This reflects the observation made above, that action should spring from assembly rather than the other way round, a point that has been particularly emphasised by Pope Benedict. His first encyclical constantly emphasised how the practical manifestation of love was absolutely intrinsic to the Church's nature. Thus:

> Love for widows and orphans, prisoners, and the sick and needy of every kind, is as essential to her as the ministry of the sacraments and preaching of the Gospel. The Church cannot neglect the service of charity any more than she can neglect the Sacraments and the Word.[53]

And again:

> For the Church, charity is not a kind of welfare activity which could equally well be left to others, but is a part of her nature, an indispensable expression of her very being.[54]

And again:

> The Church can never be exempted from practising charity as an organized activity of believers.[55]

However, he has been equally clear that this activity must result from the prior state of "the Church, or Churches … truly be[ing] themselves."[56] Thus, as Cardinal Ratzinger, he wrote:

> Christians must not allow themselves to be downgraded to a mere means for making society moral … still less should they want to justify themselves through the usefulness of their social works. The more the Church understands herself, first and foremost as the institute for social progress, the more the social vocations dry up … vocations that flourished so much when the Church still looked essentially to God … What the Church must first do, decisively, what is her very own: she must fulfil the task on which her identity is based, to make God known and to proclaim His Kingdom.[57]

The fourth element of the Church's public life as seen in Luke 1 to 5, public confrontation, is rather less evident in Catholic social teaching, a fact which may surprise those fed on a diet of Catholic-related "controversies", such as gay-adoption, contraception, abortion and euthanasia. Nevertheless, such confrontation or, more accurately, the potential for it, is evident in two ways.

First, there is potential for confrontation between the public authorities and the Church should the former decide to outlaw what the latter deems to be intrinsic to its very existence. This was a point Cardinal Cormac Murphy-O'Connor made in his 2007 Corbishley Lecture:

> My fear is that, under the guise of legislating for what is said to be tolerance, we are legislating for intolerance. Once this begins, it is hard to see where it ends. While decrying religion as dogmatic, is dogma to prevail in the public square, forcing to the margins the legitimate expression and practice of genuine religious conviction?[58]

Second, there is potential for confrontation the other way round, as a result of what the *Compendium of Social Doctrine of the Church* calls "the [Church's] task … of denunciation":

> [The Church's] social doctrine also entails a duty to denounce, when sin is present: the sin of injustice and violence that in different ways moves through society … By denunciation, the Church's social doctrine becomes judge and defender of unrecognized and violated rights, especially those of the poor, the least and the weak.[59]

The language may be less muscular than that used by the Evangelical Alliance in its *Faith and Nation* report but the emphasis is the same. If the Church is to be true to itself, there may arise times in which it finds itself in unsolicited but unavoidable confrontation with the public authorities, just as the earliest disciples did.

conclusion

Christianity has long suffered from and needs to guard against a theocratic temptation. That recognised, the claim that if you give Christians a public foothold they will end up dominating the entire public square is disingenuous and unjustifiable. Theology and history both testify against it, as does the evidence from every mainstream Christian tradition currently operating in Britain.

We have briefly explored three of these in this chapter: Anglicanism, through the lectures of the current Archbishop of Canterbury; the Free Church tradition, through a number of denominational and inter-denominational publications; and Roman Catholicism, through the wealth of papal encyclicals, Church councils and other documents. We have argued that although there are subtle differences in these three positions, the view of Christianity's public role that each espouses maps well on to that of the earliest Church, as outlined in the opening chapters of the Acts of the Apostles.

The Church's primary public task is that of proclamation, telling the story of Christ in a way that connects with the audience of the moment. "Telling" does not mean using words alone, however, and this public proclamation is inseparable from the job of public assembly, gathering as a community that *visibly* demonstrates what living in communion, with God and each other, should and can be like. From these practices of public proclamation and public assembly there should naturally spring a hunger for public action, the feeding, clothing, housing and healing that marked the Church's life from the time when the first disciples followed Jesus.

None of these acts seeks to be or is intrinsically confrontational but each might, for various contingent reasons, antagonise the powers that be, making public confrontation the last, undesired but unavoidable element in the Church's public life.

> *The Church's primary public task is that of proclamation, telling the story of Christ in a way that connects with the audience of the moment.*

The extent of that public confrontation will depend, in large part, on the nature of the public authorities against which the Church finds itself standing, and it is this tension, such as it might be, between Church and state, that also lies at the heart of the question central to this essay.

If the current climate of opinion among mainstream UK Christian groups is that the Church should act as a public witness - to adopt an umbrella term for its practice of public proclamation, assembly, action and confrontation - to God's love, how *officially-recognised* should that witness be? How far should it be part of official civic and political structures? Should it, in other words, take place within, without or against the state? It is to this question that we now turn.

chapter 2 - references

1   H Richard Niebuhr, *Christ and Culture* (Harper and Row, 1951)
2   Nigel G Wright, "Participating without Possessing," which provides an excellent summary of both Niebuhr's and Troeltsch's categorisations
3   Chapter 2, verses 42-47; chapter 4, verses 32-37; chapter 5, verses 12-16
4   Lesslie Newbigin, *Truth to Tell: The Gospel as Public Truth* (Eerdmans, 1991)
5   See, for example, "Convictions, Loyalties and the Secular State," The Chatham Lecture, Trinity College, Oxford, 29 October 2004; "Law, Power and Peace: Christian Perspectives on Sovereignty," David Nicholls Memorial Lecture, The University Church of St Mary the Virgin, Oxford, 29 September 2005; "Religion, culture, diversity and tolerance - shaping the new Europe," Address at the European Policy Centre, Brussels, 7 November 2005; "Church Schools: a National Vision," Keynote address to the National Anglican Schools' Conference, London, 14 March 2006; "The Church's Role in the Civic Life of the Nation," House of Lords Debate, 19 May 2006; "Secularism, Faith and Freedom," Lecture given at the Pontifical Academy of Social Sciences, Rome, 23 November 2006; "Freedom and Slavery," Wilberforce Lecture Trust, City Hall, Hull, 24 April 2007; "Christianity: Public Religion and the Common Good," St Andrew's Cathedral, Singapore, 12 May 2007; "Faith Communities in a Civil Society - Christian Perspectives," King's College, Cambridge, 10 September 2007; and, most notoriously, "Civil and Religious Law in England: a Religious Perspective," Foundation Lecture at the Royal Courts of Justice, London, 7 February 2008. All of these are available at www.archbishopofcanterbury.org
6   Rowan Williams, "Christianity: Public Religion and the Common Good"
7   Rowan Williams, "Freedom and Slavery"
8   Rowan Williams, "Christianity: Public Religion and the Common Good"
9   Rowan Williams, "Church Schools: a National Vision"
10 Rowan Williams, "Religion, culture, diversity and tolerance - shaping the new Europe"
11 Address given on the announcement that he is to be the 104th Archbishop of Canterbury, http://news.bbc.co.uk/1/hi/uk/2146359.stm
12 Rowan Williams, "Religion, culture, diversity and tolerance - shaping the new Europe"
13 Rowan Williams, "Christianity: Public Religion and the Common Good"
14 Rowan Williams, "Convictions, Loyalties and the Secular State"
15 Rowan Williams, "Convictions, Loyalties and the Secular State"
16 Rowan Williams, "Convictions, Loyalties and the Secular State"
17 Rowan Williams, "Christianity: Public Religion and the Common Good"
18 Rowan Williams, "Convictions, Loyalties and the Secular State"
19 Rowan Williams, "Christianity: Public Religion and the Common Good"
20 Rowan Williams, "Secularism, Faith and Freedom"
21 Rowan Williams, "Freedom and Slavery"
22 Rowan Williams, "Freedom and Slavery"
23 Rowan Williams, "Freedom and Slavery"
24 Rowan Williams, "Freedom and Slavery"
25 Rowan Williams, "Convictions, Loyalties and the Secular State"; "Church Schools: a National Vision"
26 "Speaking for the Baptist Union of Great Britain: Finding our voice on public issues," http://www.baptist.org.uk/news_media/docs/speaking-for-bugb.pdf
27 The Evangelical Alliance also represents Christians from other, e.g Anglican, denominations, of course.
28 David Hilborn (ed.), *Movement for Change: Evangelical Perspectives on Social Transformation*, (Paternoster, 2004); *Faith and Nation: Report of a Commission of Inquiry to the UK Evangelical Alliance*, Evangelical Alliance, 2006. This section also draws on information from "Speaking for the Baptist Union of Great Britain: Finding our voice on public issues;" A Methodist Statement on Political Responsibility, Adopted by the Methodist Conference, 1995; www.baptist.org.uk www.urc.org.uk www.salvationarmy.org.uk www.methodist.org.uk and www.jointpublicissues.org.uk

29 "A Methodist Statement on Political Responsibility, Adopted by the Methodist Conference," 1995, para. 61

30 *Faith and Nation*, pp. 93,149

31 *Faith and Nation*, p. 23

32 "Speaking for the Baptist Union of Great Britain: Finding our voice on public issues"

33 *Movement for Change*, p. 52

34 *Movement for Change*, p. 52

35 *Movement for Change*, p. 47

36 *Movement for Change*, p. 25

37 *Movement for Change*, p. 48

38 "A Methodist Statement on Political Responsibility, Adopted by the Methodist Conference," 1995, para. 56

39 www.urc.org.uk

40 Jonathan Wynne-Jones, "Christians ask if force is needed to protect their religious values," *Sunday Telegraph*, 5 November 2006. The EA's response can be found at http://www.eauk.org/media/responsetotelegraph.cfm

41 *Faith and Nation*, p. 122

42 *Faith and Nation*, pp. 122-23

43 Pontifical Council for Justice and Peace, *Compendium of the Social Doctrine of the Church;* John Paul II, *Centesimus Annus;* Pope Benedict XVI, *Deus Caritas Est* and *Spe Salvi; The Common Good and the Catholic Church's Social Teaching: A statement by the Catholic Bishops' Conference of England and Wales, 1996;* Cardinal Cormac Murphy-O'Connor, "Religion and the Public Forum," Corbishley Lecture, 28 March 2007, Westminster Cathedral Hall; "Faith in Europe?" Lecture Series: 25 May 2005: Cardinal Cormac Murphy-O'Connor: "The Church in Europe," Westminster Cathedral, 25 May 2005

44 *Compendium of the Social Doctrine of the Church*, 424

45 John Paul II, *Centesimus Annus*, 46-47

46 Benedict XVI, *Deus Caritas Est*, 28

47 Cormac Murphy-O'Connor, "The Church in Europe"

48 John Paul II, *Centesimus Annus*, 51

49 Cormac Murphy-O'Connor, "The Church in Europe"

50 *Compendium of the Social Doctrine of the Church*, 81

51 Cormac Murphy-O'Connor, "The Church in Europe"

52 Cormac Murphy-O'Connor, "The Church in Europe"

53 Benedict XVI, *Deus Caritas Est*, 22

54 Benedict XVI, *Deus Caritas Est*, 25

55 Benedict XVI, *Deus Caritas Est*, 29

56 Josef Ratzinger, *Turning Point for Europe?* (Ignatius Press, 1994), p. 173

57 *Turning Point for Europe?* pp. 173-74

58 Cormac Murphy-O'Connor, "Religion and the Public Forum"

59 Compendium of the Social Doctrine of the Church, 81

public or "political"?

Philip Howard is a man with an ASBO.

For over ten years he walked the length of Oxford Street, carrying a megaphone and telling people to "be a winner, not a sinner". Then, in May 2006, after numerous complaints and several attempts to moderate his behaviour, Westminster City Council took legal action.

They won. Horseferry Road Magistrates' Court banned Mr Howard from using any "amplification device" in the area bounded by Marble Arch, Regent Street and Portman Square for three years. Oxford Street is once again safe to visit.

At about the same time, Rowan Williams was contributing to a House of Lords debate on Assisted Dying for the Terminally Ill. As Archbishop of Canterbury, Dr Williams has an automatic right to sit in the second chamber, a right that he frequently exercises. As Archbishop, he also plays a pivotal role in various national events, not least the Coronation, during which he places the crown on the monarch's head.

The fact that both Mr Howard and Dr Williams are engaged in Christian "public witness" highlights the problem with that phrase. What, in practical terms, does it mean? What form should Christian "public witness" take?

Mr Howard's indiscriminate megaphone preaching is a form of Christian public witness, as are Rowan Williams' rather more sophisticated public lectures on politics, society and culture. Norman Kember, the British peace activist abducted in Iraq in 2005 was engaged in a form of Christian public witness, as were the British army chaplains working there at the same time. The four Catholics who dug graves outside the Ministry of Defence on 28 December 2004 to protest against the Iraq war were engaged in a form of Christian public witness, as were the Anglican bishops who spoke against the war in the House of Lords. The hundreds who gathered in Westminster Cathedral to hear Cardinal Cormac Murphy-O'Connor's lecture series on "Faith in Europe?" were attending a form of public witness, as were those who gathered outside Parliament 18 months later to protest against the Sexual Orientation Regulations (SORs).

At first glance, the sheer breadth of activities that might be termed "public witness" appears to render the term meaningless. That first glance is misleading, however, as much of this apparent diversity is due to the *range* of issues under discussion. Christian public witness will cover everything: education, criminal justice, international debt, media ethics, sexual ethics, war, economics, international relations, and much else besides. We would be foolish to expect anything but a variety of forms of engagement.

The range of topics only accounts for some of the diversity, however. In particular, it leaves open the key question: how closely associated with the "governing authorities" should that witness be? Should Christian witness be "merely" *public*, in the sense of operating in a space to which we all have access, or should it be *"political"*, in the sense of operating within that part of public space that is the site of the "governing authorities"?

This is an important and easily misunderstood distinction. "Political", in the sense we are using it here, does not mean relating to politics or policies. On the contrary, a "merely" public action, like that of the MoD Four or the SORs protestors, can be very political in this latter sense of the word. Rather, "political" here means working with the governing authorities, whether providing welfare services, ministering to the armed forces, scrutinising legislation or crowning the head of state.

The distinction between public and "political" is the difference between a church that proclaims, assembles and acts where everyone can see it, and one that does the same working with or sometimes within the governing authorities. It is the difference between independent schools set up and run according to a Christian ethos, and voluntary-aided church schools, in which Church and state work together to fund and operate the school. It is the difference between the local church running a soup-kitchen and the same church partnering with statutory authorities to deliver welfare provision. In its acutest form, it is the difference between a Catholic priest protesting against the Iraq war outside the MoD and an Anglican bishop doing the same inside the House of Lords.

Not every form of witness will fall neatly into either the "public" or the "political" category, of course. The Archbishop of Canterbury's public lectures are not "political" in this sense, but the attention they attract is due, in large part, to his official, i.e. "political" role as head of the established Church. The SORs demonstrations were certainly not "political" in this sense, protesting as they were *against* the government, but they were legally permitted and they sought, ultimately, to change government policy. The actions of the MoD Four, by comparison, were neither legally permitted nor attempted to change government policy, which had already sent troops to war. There are different kinds of public witness, just as there are different kinds of "political" witness. The boundaries between the two are blurred.

That recognised, these concepts of the (merely) public and ("officially") political do capture the essence of the dilemma. In concrete terms, should Christian public witness be enacted *without* or even *against* the governing authorities, as in the case of the SORs protests, Norman Kember and the MoD Four, or should it take place *with* or *within* them, as with army chaplains or bishops in the Lords? Should it be public or "political"?

theological guidelines: flexibility and adaptation

Frustratingly, neither Scripture nor tradition gives a particularly clear steer on the answer.

Perhaps not surprisingly, given the various political milieux in which early Israel found itself, the Old Testament describes a number of different modes of (what we might, anachronistically, term) "public witness", none of which appears to be normative. These vary from forms of theocracy described in chapter 1, during the centuries of Israel's self-government, to the rather more quiescent community life of the post-exilic period, which focused on worship, waiting, obeying and questioning.[1]

The New Testament documents were composed over a much shorter period, although one in which there was as much (if not more) disagreement over the issue of "public witness", meaning, at that time, how the Jews of Palestine should respond to the occupying authorities. In the words of New Testament scholar James Dunn:

> *Should Christian public witness be enacted without or even against the governing authorities, or should it take place with or within them?*

> Second Temple Judaism was made up of a number of more fragmented and diverse interest groups. They all shared a common heritage … but they expressed that common heritage in different ways.[2]

This is likely to have left a mark on the earliest Church, which Dunn sees as:

> a more or less unbroken spectrum across a wide front from conservative judaizers at one end to radical Gentile Christians at the other.[3]

It is not clear whether this diversity influenced the earliest Church's understanding of what form their public witness should take, although the odds must be that it did. Certainly there are some New Testament texts that advocate what appears to be a cooperative attitude towards the public authorities (many of which we have already encountered: 1 Timothy 2.1-2; Titus 3.1; 1 Peter 2.13-14; Romans 13.1-7), and others that suggest a more subversive approach, in which Christians should work outside, perhaps even undermining, the official authorities (e.g. Luke 4.5-8; Luke 22.25-26; John 18.33-37; 1 Corinthians 1.18-2.16; Revelation 13).

Such a heterogeneous approach is reflected in the teachings of the Church fathers. Tertullian, writing at the turn of the third century, passionately advocated the separation of Church and state (again, an anachronistic phrase). For him, it was simply inconceivable that military service, for example, could be compatible with Christianity. By accepting military office, "the line is crossed in transferring one's name from the camp of light to the camp of darkness."[4]

Conversely, little more than a century later, Eusebius of Caesarea could proclaim in a speech at the dedication of the Holy Sepulchre Church in Jerusalem:

> by the express appointment of the same God, two roots of blessing, the Roman empire and the doctrine of Christian piety sprang up together for the benefit of men.[5]

The difference in these seemingly diametrically opposed views lies, of course, in the historical shift between the early third and mid-fourth centuries. Tertullian lived and wrote at a time when martyrdom at the hands of the state was a genuine threat, Eusebius at a time when persecution of Christians was over, the empire no longer officially idolatrous, and the supremacy of Christ officially recognised. The benefit of centuries of hindsight tempts us to scoff at Eusebius's credulousness, his naivety in believing that the conversion of Constantine should transform the Roman Empire into the Kingdom of God. But that would be a mistake. The shift in moral orientation of the Roman Empire between the time of Tertullian and of Eusebius may not have been as great as the latter imagined or wished, but it was still real and significant. It is this, more than any sudden shift in political theology, that led to the greater willingness to work with and within official political structures.

This tension has existed, to a greater or lesser extent, throughout the Church's history and remains a live issue today. Whereas some Christians insist that true Christian public witness demands wholesale withdrawal from state structures, others claim that such separation is neither necessary nor sensible, and are content for a varying degree of collaboration.

To be clear, this diversity of opinion is not about *whether* the Church should witness - proclaiming, assembling around and acting out the gospel story - in public, but rather *how* it should do so, and, in particular, how it should do so in relation to the existing public authorities.

Such diversity and, in particular, the inability of either Scripture or tradition to offer a clear steer on the question of how "political" the Church's witness should be, may tempt many to throw up their arms in resignation: there is no blueprint and few guidelines, so we might as well give up trying.

Yet, to do this would be a mistake, as it would overlook the fact that the theological openness regarding this question itself constitutes a substantive point, from which two key conclusions can be drawn.

The first is that, although some positions have rather better theological credentials than others (i.e. neither theocracy nor privatisation are legitimate options), the diversity of ways in which the Church can and has conducted its public witness suggests that there is no blueprint for that witness, no model for how close to or distant from the public authorities the Church should operate. We should not, in other words, seek after the demonstrably and eternally correct model for the Church's public witness, but rather *for the most appropriate one in the given circumstances.*

This first point leads directly on to the second. The reason why there is no blueprint for the Church's public witness is that the states in which it finds itself operating will vary enormously in nature and this will dictate the extent to which Christian public witness should be within, without or against the state. Put simplistically, the more that the state in question reflects the political values of the Kingdom of God, the more acceptable it would be for Christian public witness to work with official public structures; the less it does, the less acceptable.[6]

> *As history repeatedly informs us, whether a state is officially Christian or not may make precious little difference to its structures, values and activities.*

It was this distinction that lay behind Tertullian's and Eusebius's apparently very different attitudes to the nature of public witness. The latter, unlike the former, lived in an age in which the state had crossed a crucial threshold and now recognised Christ as Lord. As far as he was concerned (although it should be noted that Eusebius was a rather extreme advocate of this position) that made officially endorsed public witness legitimate.

It is important to recognise that this is not simply a question of whether a state is Christian or not. A state would not necessarily have to be officially Christian for the Church's public witness to occur within official structures. Indeed, as history repeatedly informs us, whether a state is officially Christian or not may make precious little difference to its structures, values and activities.

Rather, it is a question of the state's official moral orientation, the concept of good that underpins its structures, values and activities, which should determine how "political" the Church's public witness should be.

It is perhaps this question of the state's moral orientation that underlies the apparently diverse attitudes to the authorities (and, by implication, to the Church's willingness to work within, without or against them) that is in evidence in the New Testament.

It is, for example, interesting to note that those passages that give a reason why Christians should "submit … to the governing authorities" (e.g. Romans 13; 1 Peter 2; 1 Timothy 2) do so in terms of those authorities' duty to "punish those who do wrong and to commend those who do right … that we may live peaceful and quiet lives." (1 Peter 2.14; 1 Timothy 2.2) In other words, the moral orientation of the state under scrutiny in these passages is towards social order and justice, objectives that are consonant with the Kingdom of God.

In contrast to this, those passages that suggest a more negative attitude to the state (and, by implication, non-engagement or more antagonistic forms of engagement) highlight not its obligation to maintain order and justice but rather its supposedly self-validating authority, its exercise of power, and its treatment of Christians:

> The devil … said to him … "I will give you all their authority and splendour, for it has been given to me," [Luke 4.6] … The kings of the Gentiles lord it over them … But you are not to be like that, [Luke 22.25-26] … You would have no power over me if it were not given to you from above, [John 19.11] … The beast … was given power to make war against the saints and to conquer them. And he was given authority over every tribe, people, language and nation. [Revelation 13.5-7]

The fact that these very different perceptions of and, therefore, attitudes to the *same* state co-exist in the New Testament point to the fact that very few states are likely to exhibit a single, obvious, incontestable moral orientation. Underlying concepts of the good will be complex and unclear and it may not be obvious how far they are consonant with the Church's. This, as we shall see, lies at the heart of the debate over the Church's role in modern Britain.

chapter 3 - references

1   Christopher Wright, *Living as the People of God* (IVP, 1983), p. 7

2   James DG Dunn, *The Partings of the Ways: Between Christianity and Judaism and their Significance for the Character of Christianity* (SCM, 1991; 2nd ed. 2006), p. 16

3   Dunn, *Partings of the Ways*, p. 6

4   Tertullian, "The Military Chaplet," in O'Donovan and O'Donovan, *Irenaeus*, p. 27

5   Eusebius of Caesarea, From a Speech on the Dedication of the Holy Sepulchre Church, in O'Donovan and O'Donovan, *Irenaeus*, p. 58

6   This, of course, begs the difficult question, what precisely are the "political values of the Kingdom of God"? Theos is currently working with the Kirby Laing Institute for Christian Ethics on a volume of essays exploring this

moral orientations

Bishop Polycarp was an old man when he was executed by the Roman Empire. Bishop of Smyrna in what is now modern-day Turkey, Polycarp was the victim of a growing persecution of Christians in the second century. He is the first Christian martyr, outside the New Testament, of whose death we have an authentic account.[1]

Arrested and brought before the Roman governor, he was given a stark choice: either curse the name of Christ, declare that "Caesar is Lord", and swear "by the Luck of the Emperor", or face death.

His response was simple, yet highlighted the fundamental disconnect between the moral orientation - the underlying concept of public good - of the early Christians and the Roman "state" in which they lived:

> I've served him [Christ] for eighty-six years, and he's never done me any wrong; so how can I blaspheme my King who saved me?

Superficially, a rather emotive response, Polycarp's words were profoundly and antagonistically political. In the Roman mind, Caesar was King and Saviour: hence the shibboleth Polycarp was required to utter. In the Christian one, Christ was Lord. Even if the two world-views were identical in every other respect (and, of course, they were not) this constituted an insurmountable difference, a massive "wall of separation" between Church and "state".

The cult of Emperor worship was better established at the time of Polycarp's execution, probably in AD 156, than it was at the time of Paul's, around 90 years earlier, but it was nonetheless a genuine phenomenon in the first century, especially around the eastern parts of the empire. Indeed, during St Paul's lifetime, the Imperial cult was the fastest growing religion in the Mediterranean world.[2] For all the circumstantial differences between the mid-second and the mid-first centuries, the idolatrous nature of the "state" in which Christians lived was, by and large, a constant.

And yet, as we have already noted, even recognising this fact the New Testament still contains a number of passages in which Peter and Paul write *positively* about the public authorities, highlighting their duty to punish wrongdoers and to maintain order.

This should give us reason to pause. If any state demanded that the Church should act *against* it, surely the Roman one did. Idolatrous, violent, oppressive, Imperial: surely there was nothing good in it? Surely Christians were required actively to undermine and challenge its authority?

The uncomfortable answer presented by the New Testament is "No". The early Christians were hardly supine in the face of public authority, but nor were they political "revolutionaries" as we popularly understand the word. Instead, both they and the New Testament documents recognise that not even the Imperial Roman authorities were monochromatically wicked. For all their violence and idolatry, they still exercised a legitimate role in maintaining order and justice. The moral orientation of the state was complex.

If it were complex for first-century Rome, how much more complex is it for twenty-first century Britain? The examples of Polycarp, Paul and the empire in which they lived suggest strongly that, when thinking through this question as it relates to contemporary Britain, we would do better to talk about the state's various moral orientations than about its singular moral orientation.

beyond public opinion

Before we do so, however, it is important to clear up a common mistake.

Living in a democracy, we sometimes use the phrases "British state" and "British society" interchangeably, assuming that the moral orientation of the state must be the same as that of the people who vote in its government. It is not, as several well-known examples indicate.

The death penalty for murder was abolished in Britain in 1965, although it remained on the statute book for a few other offences until 1998. Despite this, and according to the annual British Social Attitudes (BSA) survey, the weight of British public opinion has consistently been in support of the death penalty in certain circumstances. In 2005, when BSA asked respondents whether they agreed that "for some crimes, the death penalty is the most appropriate sentence", 58% either agreed or agreed strongly and only 26% disagreed/disagreed strongly. This represents a shift from 73% agreeing versus 19% disagreeing when the same question was asked in 1986, but it still indicates majority public approval for the death penalty "for some crimes".[3]

Conversely, again according to the British Social Attitudes survey, "the current law that prohibits assisted dying seems to be at odds with public opinion."[4] Four in five people think that a doctor should be legally permitted to end a patient's life if that person has "an incurable and painful illness, from which they will die".[5] As with capital punishment, the majority of the population's moral orientation in this matter is not reflected by the state's.

People are often indignant at facts like these, citing them as a reason for political apathy and disenchantment. However, a moment's reflection should tell us that, short of government by a continuous string of binding referendums - a costly, fragmentary and unattractive option that swiftly degenerates into government by newspaper editorial - the only realistic way of handling the volatile and diverse conceptions of the good held by a plural public is through some system of representation.

The point of this is to head off the ubiquitous "who voted for you?" criticism that plagues every debate about the public good. In the *Today* programme debate cited at the start of this essay, Lord Harrison, commenting on the role of prison chaplains, remarked that he was "not aware that our prisons are overcrowded exclusively with regular churchgoers".

Prison chaplaincy, like other public goods, exists not because it precisely mirrors public values but because it embodies a concept of the good to which the public assents.

This view demonstrates this popular fallacy: that a public good, such as prison chaplaincy, is only justified if it clearly reflects the values of the public it serves, in this instance, prisoners or, perhaps, taxpayers. In reality, prison chaplaincy, like other public goods, exists not because it precisely mirrors public values but because it embodies a concept of the good to which the public assents.

This does not, of course, mean that there is *no* connection between the state's conception of the good and its public's. There clearly is, as we shall note below. The fact is, however, that it is more complex, attenuated and buffered than the simple "who voted for you?" argument recognises.

The key to understanding the moral orientation(s) of the state, therefore, is to note public opinion polls and then to go beyond them and look at the concepts of the good which, through the vehicle of public opinion, become embodied in public policy, law and even the constitution.

moral orientations: the historical influence

There are, in essence, two reasons why we should be advised to talk of the moral orientations (as opposed to orientation) of the state, each of which, in its own way, sheds light on the nature of those orientations. The first, analysed here, deals with historical considerations, whilst the second, explored in the following section, looks at contemporary ones.

The fact, noted above, that there is a disconnect between public opinion and the concept of the good embodied in the state does not mean that opinion polls are irrelevant, or that there is *no* connection between the public's concept of the good and the state's. That connection may not be direct but it is nonetheless real. In a representative democracy, at least in theory, public opinion will *gradually* shape the concept of the good that underlies the state.

This need not be a one-way process. Electorates often vote into power political parties whose policies subsequently shape and direct the electorate's opinions, as has happened with race and gender legislation since the 1960s. Governments can form public opinion just as much as filter it.

However, the basic pattern in a representative democracy is of a political process that is sensitive to public opinion, and turns that opinion, or elements of it, into law which itself subsequently shapes public opinion. The whole iterative process is complicated, messy and can take considerable time, a fact that is crucial for understanding the moral orientations of the modern British state.

The time-lag *can* be short. At a trivial level, public panic over a series of canine attacks in the early 1990s resulted in the notoriously rushed 1991 Dangerous Dogs Act, which embodied in law the public's somewhat frenzied fear of big, angry dogs. At a less trivial level, the Jubilee Drop the Debt campaign, totally unknown in 1991, managed, against the odds, to change government policy and secure significant debt cancellation for many lower-income nations within little more than a decade. Both are examples of the public's idea of the good influencing that of the state in an unusually short time.

In many other cases, the process takes rather longer. The anger voiced by many on the "left" in the recent euthanasia debate reflects their frustration at what they see as an unacceptable time lag: how can the state refuse to recognise and endorse contemporary (majority) public opinion in favour of a moral understanding of the value of life that was predominant twenty or thirty years ago. It seems patently unjust and undemocratic to outlaw "assisted dying" if the majority of the present population favours it.

Those expressing this outrage, however, tend not to mention an even greater disconnect between public opinion and law, namely that over the issue of capital punishment. This is cited, commonly by those on the "right", as a classic example of the state's concept of the good not so much lagging behind the population's, as completely ignoring it.[6]

The moral orientations of the British state, then, are not simply mirror images of its public's, but rather the result of the slow, filtered accumulation of public opinion - usually majority opinion, occasionally minority opinion, never unanimous opinion - over many years.

The state acts not as a puppet, operated by whims of contemporary opinion, but as a living being whose body is shaped and marked by current *and previous* conceptions of the good. Those marks are by no means indelible - laws can be repealed and conventions changed - but they are often very deeply ingrained. The state is, to a greater or lesser extent, an inheritor of the mentality and world-view of earlier times.[7] As the philosopher Charles Taylor has written in a different context, "our past is sedimented in our present".[8]

It is this that lies at the heart of the first reason why we should talk of the state's moral orientations: because at any one time, the state embodies concepts of the good that are decades or even centuries old.

constitutional artefacts

Nowhere is this more apparent than in evaluating the Christian influence on British public life. Unpalatable as it is to some, however plural, nominally Christian or quasi-secular it is today, the British nation has very definite and very deep Christian roots, which continue to feed the modern state.

It will inevitably be important to clear away some misunderstandings at this point. The British state was never Christian in the sense of fully embodying the values of the Kingdom of God. Similarly, the British people were never wholly Christian, either in the sense of the previous sentence or even in the looser senses of, for example, biblical knowledge or church attendance.[9] Nevertheless, from the seventh century onwards, Christianity has been the dominant, if not quite the only feature on our mental landscape. In the words of the House of Lords Select Committee on Religious Offences in England and Wales:

> [T]he constitution of the United Kingdom is rooted in faith - specifically the Christian faith exemplified by the established status of the Church of England … The United Kingdom is not a secular state.[10]

It is this immovable fact that lies at the heart of many cultural and constitutional artefacts, some of which were mentioned in the introduction. Why does the national flag centre on the Christian cross?[11] Why do we have patron saints? Why does the national anthem begin with the words "God save"? Why do we have public holidays at Christmas and Easter? Why does the academic year divide into three terms? Why do some institutions call these terms Michaelmas, Hilary and Trinity? Why do the blasphemy laws exist? Why do they pertain only to the Christian religion? Why are British coins inscribed with the letters "DG REG FD"?[12] Why does the British tax year start on 6 April?[13] Why do 26 Anglican bishops sit in the House of Lords? Why are so many NHS hospitals named after Christian saints? Why does the figure of Jesus Christ adorn the highest point of the upper arch at the entrance to the Royal Courts of Justice in the Strand? Why is he flanked by statues of Solomon and Moses?[14] Why are court witnesses asked to swear an oath on a holy book at all and the Bible specifically, as opposed to all being required simply to make a solemn affirmation? Why does the 1988 Education Act insist that "all pupils in attendance at a maintained school shall on each school day take part in an act of collective worship"? Why does the business of Parliament each day begin with prayers? Why does the Queen's speech end with the phrase, "I pray that the blessing of Almighty God may rest upon your counsels"? Why do the Official Oath, Judicial Oath and the Oath of Allegiance end, "So help me God"? Why does the text of the accession declaration require the monarch to "solemnly and sincerely in the presence of God profess, testify and declare that [he/she is] a faithful Protestant"? Why is the Coronation based around a service of Holy Communion held at Westminster Abbey? Why does the Archbishop of Canterbury officiate? Why does he present the monarch with a Bible and anoint him/her with consecrated oil? Why does the Coronation oath require the monarch to "maintain the Laws of God and the true profession of the Gospel [and] the Protestant Reformed Religion established by law"? Why is "a person who is a Roman Catholic or marries a Roman Catholic ... excluded from inheriting, possessing or enjoying the Crown"?

> From the seventh century onwards, Christianity has been the dominant, if not quite the only feature on our mental landscape.

To catalogue this list of cultural and constitutional artefacts is not to imply that each is somehow "right". Some people object to the current formulation of the blasphemy laws; many more to their very existence. Some object to the presence of 26 Anglican bishops in the House of Lords; others to the presence of any. Many people, and not just Roman Catholics, object to the Protestant succession.

The fact of disagreement is not under debate. Rather, the list is to remind us that the modern British state is deeply rooted in the Christian, specifically Protestant religion, and that, consequently, its moral orientation cannot but be profoundly shaped by those specifically Christian *historical* conceptions of the good. When Peter Hitchens said in his *Today* debate with Lord Harrison, "this is a Christian country, its laws, its customs, from the Coronation service to the Bill of Rights are based upon Christianity," he was not burying his head in the historical sand. Rather, he was stating a fact, disagreeable as it may have been to Lord Harrison.

It would be a short but unjustified step to argue, at this point, that because the modern British state is so profoundly shaped by its Christian roots, it, therefore, has a Christian moral orientation. The picture is more complex than that and such a step ignores two important points.

The first is that simply because a state recognises the authority of Christ in ways such as those described above, it does not necessarily make its moral orientation "Christian", at least in any sense of the word that the New Testament writers would

> *Simply because a state recognises the authority of Christ, it does not necessarily make its moral orientation "Christian".*

recognise. The eighteenth century saw an established Church, four Westminster coronations, numerous bishops in the House of Lords, coins inscribed "by the grace of God", the adoption of "God save the King" as the national anthem and the flying of a Union flag based on the Christian cross, to name but a few cultural artefacts that symbolised the nation's Christian convictions. It also saw the development of a trans-Atlantic slave trade, which was supported by many Christians, and the rise of a poor, disenfranchised, urban underclass, that the established Church at least was largely disengaged from and often indifferent towards. Pointing an accusing finger at earlier ages is both easy and pointless and, in any case, quite how morally Christian a state could or should ever be is open to debate. The important point is that however *officially* Christian a state is, that will not necessarily have a significant bearing on its *actual* moral orientation.

post-, sub-, or quasi-Christian?

The second point is that, inheritors as we are of a thoroughly Christian past, British society today is less influenced by the Christian faith than at any time in the last thousand years or so.

Again, it is important to clear up misunderstandings at this point. The British Humanist Association commissioned Ipsos/MORI in 2006/07 to gauge "the levels of Humanist-related opinion that exists amongst the British population", and found that just over a third (36%) of the British population "has a Humanist outlook on life".[15] Similarly, it is commonly reported that today "only" 7-8% of the population actively belongs to any Christian denomination. Such statistics are sometimes cited to demonstrate that Britain is post-Christian.

Important as such data are they need to be integrated alongside other surveys. The 2001 Census confirmed what many smaller research samples have shown, namely that around 70% of the population claims to belong to the Christian religion. The British Social Attitudes survey, in 1998 and again in 2000, reported that roughly the same proportion claims to believe in God or a "Higher Power". The fact is that, however much the population shares "Humanist-related opinion[s]" (a notably vague phrase), the overwhelming majority is *nominally* Christian and theist.

Similarly, one needs to be careful about using the word "only" in the context of church attendance figures. If "only" 4.5 million people actively belong to a Christian denomination, what word should we use to describe the *thousands* who actively belong to secular or humanist ones? To quote the House of Lords Select Committee on Religious Offences in England and Wales again:

> [A]lthough there is little doubt that the pre-eminent role enjoyed by the established church is probably outdated … our own researches, and the evidence we heard, reinforce a view that religious belief continues to be a significant component, or even determinant, of social values, and plays a major role in the lives of a large number of the population.[16]

The view that Britain is, therefore, post-Christian is, thus, untenable. But the same must be said of the view that Britain is Christian *in the way it was when the various cultural and constitutional artefacts outlined above were laid down*. Things have changed.

cultural realities

> In 1961, suicide ceased to be a crime. This might seem a minor and obviously humane measure, but it was the beginning of the end of England as a Christian country; that is, one in which Christian ethics was reflected in law.[17]

Chief Rabbi Sir Jonathan Sacks' remark in *The Times* in October 2007 begs several important questions, not least how far Christian ethics *should* be "reflected in law" (a question on which Christians themselves seem unable to agree). Nevertheless, it makes a key observation, one that must be placed alongside the constitutional artefacts listed above: the British state is *mentally* less Christian today than at any time in the recent past.

This is a significant claim and needs justification. A great deal of post-war legislation, such as the attacks on racial discrimination, is demonstrably *more* rather than *less* Christian, reflecting, albeit silently, the Christian conviction that everyone is made "in the image of God" (Genesis 1.27) and "possesses the dignity of a person … capable of self-knowledge, of self-possession and of freely giving himself".[18]

Similarly, it is not simply the case, for example, that when the state *removes* a Christian "value" from the statute book it becomes less Christian. As we have emphasised throughout this essay, Christianity (now) recognises that Church and state have different roles to play. Blasphemy and adultery are understood by Christians to be sinful, but that does not mean they should be illegal, a distinction made by the 1957 Wolfenden report, which itself took its cue from a 1952

If "only" 4.5 million people actively belong to a Christian denomination, what word should we use to describe the thousands who actively belong to secular or humanist ones?

report from the Church of England Moral Welfare Council.[19] Thus, to return to Jonathan Sacks' example, just because the Church historically understood suicide to be sinful and managed to persuade British law-makers to enshrine that value in public law, the repealing of that value in 1961 did not necessarily make the state less Christian. It could, paradoxically, make it more Christian, in the sense of moving it closer to the New Testament's vision of what the state should achieve.

How, then, is the British state mentally less Christian today than, say, 50 years ago? The obvious answers - fewer people attend church, know the Christian story, or openly admit to living to the Christian ethic - fall into the state/society confusion mentioned above. Such trends will undoubtedly provide the *context* for the state's moral orientation, but they do not mark that orientation in themselves.

A better answer would be gleaned from studying particular laws or policies, but even this has its problems. The laws on a statute book are, as we have noted, often legacies from earlier and mentally different ages, making them a hazardous guide to our current moral orientation. In addition, and as we shall note below, such laws may not be joined-up, thereby offering a confusing picture. Finally, laws do not, as a rule, display or discuss their underlying conception of the good. That is not their business.

Instead, a better (if still problematic) way of understanding current political conceptions of the public good is to explore the presuppositions, in particular those relating to the human person, which underpin legislation.

This will, inevitably, sound somewhat vague. Neither governments nor legislative programmes are eager to articulate the anthropological presuppositions underlying their thought, even assuming those presuppositions are recognised and coherent. Similarly, there is nothing to suggest that such presuppositions will be consistent with one another.

Nevertheless, such presuppositions still exist. Sacks' example, quoted above, does point to a genuine post-war shift in the state's understanding of the human person and what constitutes their "good", even if that was not articulated as part of the act itself.

That understanding, like so many others, relates to the issue of personal autonomy.

autonomy

My starting point is that from the time of Magna Carta, to the civil wars and revolutions of the seventeenth century, through to the liberalism of Victorian Britain and the widening and deepening of democracy and fundamental rights throughout the last century, there has been a British tradition of liberty - what one writer has called our "gift to the world". [20]

Gordon Brown has spoken a great deal about liberty, both as Chancellor and as Prime Minister. According to Brown, "the restriction of arbitrary power and the empowerment of the individual ... [has been the] golden thread" throughout British history, and needs to remain a guiding light today.

Few would disagree, although there is often something left unsaid in all the liberty rhetoric. Brown himself, in his speech on liberty at the University of Westminster in October 2007, gestured in this direction by quoting the nineteenth century French historian and political thinker Alexis de Tocqueville:

> *The thrust towards political liberty ... has long been balanced by a culture that has prevented liberty from descending into "the selfishness of extreme libertarianism".*

I enjoyed ... in England ... a union between the religious and the political world, between public and private virtue, between Christianity and liberty.

The thrust towards political liberty - freedom *from* public authorities to decide one's own fate - has long been balanced by a culture that has prevented liberty from descending into what Brown called "the selfishness of extreme libertarianism". [21] That culture has emphasised the ties that bind over the attractions of personal autonomy. It has been both social, shaped largely by the nation's Christian culture, and economic, with socialism and the Trades Union movement reining in the worst excesses of *laissez-faire* capitalism.

These counterbalancing forces were more or less successful in passing their particular conceptions of the good into law between the mid-nineteenth and mid-twentieth centuries, but the post-war period witnessed the erosion of both of these counterbalances. The 1960s and then the 1980s marked the end, or rather the beginning of the end, of first Christian and then socialist conceptions of the good as political justifications.

Into the void has stepped the concept of the person as an autonomous individual, which has long motivated the struggle for political liberty that Brown rightly lauds. This emphatically does not mean that Britain has crossed some libertarian Rubicon and that all policy decisions are now founded on the idea of unencumbered personal liberty. [22] As we shall note below, the picture is rather more complex than that. It does, however, mean that we are increasingly inclined to see human independence and personal liberty as our guiding lights in social and economic spheres as well as the more narrowly political one.

Thus, we find the language of choice, freedom and rights used by both the "liberal left" and the "conservative right".[23] The entitlement to abortion and to euthanasia, popular with the liberal left, is justified by the argument from choice: we should have the right to choose what to do with our bodies. Conversely, the introduction of market mechanisms in public services, in particular in education and health, a cause more popular with the conservative right, is premised on the belief that patients and parents should be able to choose the services they use, rather than have them handed to them, and that their exercise of choice will, in turn, improve the efficiency of those services.

The gradual devaluing of marriage in public policy and rhetoric over recent decades, a trend associated with the liberal left, has much to do with the conviction that adults should be able to choose whatever lifestyle they wish without encountering vocal or economic "judgement". Conversely, the deregulation of credit or Sunday trading, legislation associated with the conservative right, is premised on the idea that people are "adult" and should, therefore, have the freedom to choose when they want to borrow money or shop.

The restriction of bad language, sexual content, violent material and blasphemy on broadcast media tends to be more unpopular with those on the liberal left, as it is commonly judged to be an unacceptable infringement of personal liberty. Conversely, restricting car use, through direct taxation, congestion or road-charging, is usually more unpopular with those on the conservative right, seen as an unacceptable infringement of personal mobility. In each case, the argument is that people should be free to choose as they see fit, an argument that is based on the assumption of human independence.

It is easy to see why this conception of individual autonomy should be appealing. In a society that is more culturally and morally plural today than at any time in living memory, there are obvious attractions to maximising individual freedom, so that as few people as possible have as little as possible imposed on them. However, such appeal disguises a preconception that is a potential problem for many people, not least Christians.

The principle of maximal personal liberty is foundational to the liberal political philosophy that has proved so influential in the West over recent decades, a fact reflected in the first of John Rawls' two key principles of justice:

> Each person is to have an equal right to the most extensive total system of equal basic liberties compatible with a similar system of liberty for all.[24]

This instinctively sounds appealing but, in Rawls' formulation at least, the path to this principle involves conceptualising individuals in such a way as to ignore not only their social position, but also their personal talents and their conception of the good. Since the distribution of these attributes is, according to Rawls, "arbitrary from a moral point of view," they cannot be taken into account in ordering a just society.[25]

The result, however, as communitarian critics of Rawls have often pointed out, is a political philosophy that is founded on a thoroughly non-human concept of a person - asocial, individualistic, divorced from everything that makes them a person. Such an emphasis on inviolable personal autonomy might provide the foundation for a "just" society, but at what cost?

At the risk of repetition, this tendency towards seeing personal autonomy as a maximal good does not mean the concept of good underlying the modern British state is either determinedly libertarian or is even on the road to libertarianism. The spate of "reviews" announced in 2007 - on super casinos, the reclassification of cannabis as a class C drug and extended licensing hours - reminds us that these issues are in constant flux.

Nor, similarly, does it mean that a once invariably Christian understanding of the human person was suddenly, say in 1963 or 1979, replaced with a thoroughly (socially or economically) liberal one.

Instead, it makes a less ambitious point. The concept of the good that underlies British policy, law and constitution invariably changes over time. In the post-war period, it has shifted from one that was shaped significantly by a Christian world-view, to another that places a greater emphasis on personal autonomy. This is not a wholesale rejection of the Christian understanding of the human person but, as we shall see in the concluding chapter, it does open up the potential for some tension.

moral orientations: contemporary thinking

The second reason for talking about the state's moral orientations rather than orientation will be evident from the first.

The fact that the language and logic of freedom, rights and choice are adopted and opposed by the "left" and the "right", depending on the issue in question, signifies that there is still a debate to be had. Not only is contemporary politics not shaped by a single conception of the human person and public good, but most of it is shaped by composite or compromised conceptions. There are two reasons for this, one good, the other less so.

First, as outlined above, the British political process is "designed" to prevent the monopoly of the public square by any one particular group. A society that is in any way morally plural, like modern Britain, will play host to a diversity of conceptions of the good. The processes, checks and balances within the political system are intended, in part, to prevent any one of these dominating or, rather, to prevent it from dominating beyond the extent to which it is favoured by the population at large. The political system, in other words, is designed to prevent unduly privileging certain conceptions over others.

The result is that legislation will naturally fudge together different moral orientations. Sunday legislation is a good example. On the one hand, there is a clear logic to restricting Sunday trading. This integrates consideration for employment rights, family time, local, independent retail "ecologies" (and their significant contribution to community life), and, more broadly, the value of a day in which society rests from its ceaseless "getting and spending". Ultimately, the argument is based on conceptions of the good that we might call communitarian.

On the other hand, there is a clear logic to further derestricting Sunday trading. This is based fundamentally on choice. The campaign to further deregulate Sunday trading stresses that consumers and shopworkers should have the freedom to choose when they shop and work. Indeed, its website is called mysundaymychoice.com The arguments are based on a more liberal conception of the good, which we have discussed above.

The current legislation, passed in 1994, states that stores over a certain size (in England and Wales) are allowed to open on a Sunday, but only for six hours. This was confirmed by a review in 2006. Neither stricter regulation nor further deregulation got its own way. Campaigns and, with them, different conceptions of the good are forced to compromise. Both sides - or neither - are happy.

If this deliberate fudging of moral orientations is, to some extent, necessary in a representative, plural democracy such as ours, there is a second sense in which we see different moral orientations compete against one another, only this time in a way that owes less to social reality and more to a lack of joined-up thinking.

This is most evident in big issues that stretch across sectors and departments, such as climate change. In one breath, the government can announce plans to phase out high-energy incandescent light bulbs by 2011 and, in another, suggest that by 2030 the number of passengers passing through UK airports "could, if sufficient capacity were provided, have risen to between 400 million and 600 million ... two and three times what it is today".[26]

Judging this apparent conflict as generously as possible, one might see it as an example of the kind of inevitable and, in some sense, necessary conflict noted above, where the competing visions of the good, in this case environmental protection and economic growth, result in a messy compromise. More sceptically, it reflects a situation in which a government that has talked a great deal about climate change is simply failing, or refusing, to join all its policy dots.

Similar problems affect other cross-departmental policy areas, such as childhood. The impact of spending £500 million on children's reading skills is almost bound to be dented, if not rendered wholly ineffective, by policies that weaken family life, the first and most effective educational establishment a child experiences.[27] Similarly, plans to tackle the level of teenage pregnancy or sexually-transmitted infections are thwarted by an unwillingness to limit products and advertising that objectify and sexualise children.[28]

Whether it is due to the fact that politics is the business of compromise or that government policy dots simply do not join up, it is a mistake to talk of a single moral orientation of the British state. The situation may be not so much one of confusion as of complexity, but this complexity needs to be recognised if we are to come up with a credible framework for determining the role of Christianity in twenty-first century Britain.

conclusion

The moral orientation of the modern British state is itself plural. Both for historical and contemporary reasons the state encompasses a variety of conceptions of the human person and the public good.

This will mean that when we ask the question posed in the previous chapter - how "political" as opposed to public should Christian social witness be? - the answer we receive is a frustrating but realistic, "it depends".

It depends *not* on the Church, which must proclaim, assemble and act the message of the gospel "in season and out of season", as Paul instructs Timothy. (2 Timothy 4.2) Rather, it depends on the nature of the state, and, in particular, its moral orientations - the concepts of the human person and the public good that underpin it. Because the state changes over time and its government does a variety of different, sometimes seemingly irreconcilable things, those moral orientations will be many and varied. How far should Christian witness take place within, without or against existing political structures? It depends on the nature of those political structures.

> *Both for historical and contemporary reasons the state encompasses a variety of conceptions of the human person and the public good.*

This conclusion will frustrate many who want a simple and clear-cut answer to the question. It is so much more satisfying to be able to say either "Disestablish! Privatise! Evict the bishops! Close faith schools!" or "This is a Christian country - those who don't like it can move elsewhere". Yet neither position does justice to the shifting, diverse complexity of modern British state and society.

This conclusion may not allow us to rally the troops and send them into battle for whichever cause we think right. That, in a sense, is the point of this whole essay. Bombast, polemic and demonisation are the worst ways of dealing with issues such as this.

It does, however, furnish us with a framework by means of which we can evaluate and adjudicate on the role of Christianity in modern Britain on a case-by-case basis. The final chapter explores how this might work.

chapter 4 - references

1   "The Martyrdom of Polycarp," in *Early Christian Writings: The Apostolic Fathers*, ed. A Louth (Penguin Books, 1968; rev. 1987), pp.125-35

2   NT Wright, "Paul and Caesar: A New Reading of Romans," in *A Royal Priesthood? The Use of the Bible Ethically and Politically*, ed. Craig Bartholomew et al. (Zondervan, 2002), p. 175

3   These figures can be found at www.britsocat.com

4   Elizabeth Clery, Sheila McLean and Miranda Phillips, "Quickening death: the euthanasia debate," in *British Social Attitudes: the 23rd Report: Perspectives on a changing society*, ed. Alison Park et al. (National Centre for Social Research/SAGE, 2007), pp. 35-50

5   The exact question is: "Suppose a person has a painful incurable disease. Do you think that doctors should be allowed by law to end the patient's life if the patient requests it?"

6   It is sometimes said that, in this instance, the state's conception of the good is going ahead of the public's, although how we should know what public opinion will (as opposed to should) be in 10 or 20 years' time is not always clear

7   Which can manifest itself in some long-standing and rather bizarre laws. It remains illegal, for example, in Britain to enter the Houses of Parliament wearing a suit of armour, to place a postage stamp bearing the British king or queen's image upside-down, or, dating from the time of the Puritans, to eat mince pies on Christmas Day. See http://news.bbc.co.uk/1/hi/uk/7081038.stm for other such anomalies

8   Charles Taylor, *A Secular Age* (Belknap/Harvard, 2007), p. 29

9   Surveys, both quantitative, such as the 1851 Church attendance census, and qualitative, such as the study of the religious attitudes of trench soldiers in the First World War, reveal a nation that was not only not ubiquitously religious, but often disturbingly familiar to our own. See Robin Gill, *The Myth of the Empty Church* (London: SPCK, 1993)

10 House of Lords Select Committee on Religious Offences in England and Wales, 2003, para. 132

11 An idea dating back at least to the thirteenth century in the case of the St George's flag and the eighth century in the case of the Saltire

12 Meaning "By the Grace of God, Queen and Defender of the Faith"

13 The British year historically began not on 1 January but 25 March, marking the date of Jesus' incarnation in Mary's womb (i.e. 9 months before Christmas Day). When the nation adopted the Gregorian calendar in 1752 the Inland Revenue decided to leave the date of the new tax year where it was to avoid confusing the population. They did, however, move it forward 11 days, because the year 1752/1753 was shortened by 11 days (to catch up the time lost through the old Julian calendar), so that they would avoid further angering an already incensed population by forcing them to pay a full year's tax for a year that was only 354 days long

14 For details see: http://www.hmcourts-service.gov.uk/infoabout/rcj/history.htm

15 Ipsos/MORI, "Measuring Humanist Belief Amongst The British Population": http://www.ipsos-mori.com/polls/2006/humanism.shtml

16 House of Lords Select Committee on Religious Offences in England and Wales, 2003, para. 132

17 Jonathan Sacks, "Wanted: a national culture," *The Times*, 20 October 2007

18 *Catechism of the Catholic Church*, para. 357

19 Andrew Holden, *Makers and Manners: Politics and Morality in Postwar Britain* (Politico's, 2004), p. 65

20 Gordon Brown, Speech on Liberty at University of Westminster, 25 October 2007: http://www.labour.org.uk/pm_announces_bill_of_rights

21 Brown, Speech on Liberty, 2007

22 There are many reasons for this, although one of the most influential must be that the British public itself is consistently authoritarian and, to a lesser extent, left-wing (i.e. favouring government economic intervention) in its overall values. For more information on this, see Alison Park and Paula Surridge, "Charting change in British values," in *British Social Attitudes: the 20th Report: Continuity and Change over two decades*, ed. Alison Park et al. (National Centre for Social Research/SAGE, 2003), pp. 131-60

23 There is, of course, rather more nuance and diversity within the categories of the "liberal left" and "conservative right" than is acknowledged either in this sentence or the following paragraphs. However, space prevents a more detailed discussion

24 John Rawls, *A Theory of Justice* (Harvard University Press, 1971), p. 302

25 John Rawls, *A Theory of Justice*, p. 15

26 Department for Transport, *The Future of Air Transport*, 2003, para. 2.8

27 BBC On-line, "School literacy scheme attacked", 2 November 2007: http://news.bbc.co.uk/1/hi/education/7073275.stm

28 See, for example, American Psychological Association, *Report of the APA Task Force on the Sexualization of Girls* (2007) and, more broadly, UNICEF, *Child poverty in perspective: An overview of child well-being in rich countries* (Innocenti Research Centre, Report Card 7, 2007)

neither private nor privileged: the argument from public good

This essay has come a long way from a four and a half minute debate on the *Today* programme. It is worth recapping the argument so far.

The essay took as read the idea, discussed in *Doing God*, that religious conviction was likely to play an increasingly important role in British public life. It sought to (begin to) answer the question, 'what should that be?' with specific regard to Christianity.

Chapter 1 argued that the twin answers of "all" or "nothing" - theocracy or privatisation - are no answers at all. Enforced privatisation would be counter to the spirit of a liberal, plural democracy, not to mention counter-productive. Enforced theocracy, hardly the likeliest of options, would be worse. The chapter recognised that Christianity has indeed long suffered from a theocratic temptation, but argued that, for a variety of reasons, that temptation was no longer a threat.

One of the key reasons for this was that not a single mainstream Christian leader in the UK advocates anything even approaching theocracy today. Chapter 2 explored what they *are* advocating, using the model of the earliest Church, from chapters 1 to 5 in the Acts of the Apostles, as a framework. It argued that a four-fold picture of public proclamation, public assembly, public action and public confrontation - summarised by the phrase "public witness" - best describes what the early Church did and what UK church leaders presently advocate for Christian public engagement.

The question this begged was, then, what form should that public witness assume? Chapter 3 asked whether it should be "merely" public, meaning taking place in the public square, or whether it should be more "officially" public, meaning taking place within that part of the public square that is the site of the governing authorities. Should it, in other words, be public or "political"? Referring to Christian Scripture and tradition, the chapter argued that the Christian answer to this question is deliberately open, recognising that the nature of Christian public witness will necessarily and rightly depend on the nature of the state in which the Church finds itself. The closer its moral orientation is to that of the gospel, the greater the capacity would be for cooperation, and vice versa.

Chapter 4 took up this point and proceeded to ask the key question: what, then, is the moral orientation of the modern British state? The question is deceptively simple; the answer frustratingly complex. The moral orientation - the conception of human nature and public good - which underpins any state is varied and variable. The modern British state has very deep Christian roots that still inform its working, but the moral atmosphere that society breathes and that slowly shapes the body politic, is somewhat less Christian than it was 50 years ago. In the words of one commentator:

> In 1945 criminal law largely reflected traditional Judeo-Christian morality in the context of the rapidly industrialising society of late Victorian Britain, when laws concerning abortion, marriage and divorce, the protection of children, homosexuality, alcohol and licensing were all stiffened by the rising affluence of religious, and particularly nonconformist, moral concern.[1]

No one would say the same of Britain in 2008.

Rather than being secular, however, today's atmosphere is morally and culturally plural, to an almost unprecedented degree, meaning that, even if one were to discount the complicating historical factors, it would still be impossible to talk of the (singular) moral orientation of the British state. The fact is that we must, if we are to be faithful to social reality, talk of its moral orientations, and this means that any serious evaluation of the proper nature of Christianity's public witness needs to be made on a case-by-case basis.

This chapter will give a few, brief examples of what this might look like. Before it does that, however, it needs to answer a question that has been hanging over the essay since the introduction spoke optimistically about finding common ground. Why should anyone who is not a Christian agree with the (often theological) arguments contained here?

can we agree on this?

This essay has (hopefully) been accessible both to the religious and the non-religious, but may not have been credible to the same wide audience. If not, the likely reason is the theological nature of some of its arguments. If I do not deem the Bible to be of any revelatory significance, why should I be persuaded by arguments based on it? More generally, why should Christians be the ones to pronounce on the role of Christianity in modern British public life?

It is easier to take the second of these objections first. Those of a non- or anti-Christian persuasion will naturally question the validity of Christians pronouncing on the role of Christianity in modern Britain. Yet that simply begs the question, who, other than the people involved in it, should pronounce on the public role their organisation should have? Every public body should be able to articulate what its public role should be. It would be absurd, not to mention slightly sinister, for one group to tell another what it should advocate for its public life.

That, however, is not the same as saying every group should be able to *decide* what its role will be. The Church of England may conclude, after internal deliberations, that all of its bishops should have permanent seats in the House of Lords, unlikely as that may seem. That does not mean that all of its bishops *will* have permanent seats in the House of Lords. For that to happen, a sufficiently persuasive reason would have to be made, over time, in the public square. In other words, any organisation can and should pronounce on its public role, but in political cases it is the public, in the form of its elected officials, who will *decide*.

This leads back to the first objection. The reasoning in this essay has indeed, in places, been theological, and there is no reason why those ill-disposed towards theology should be convinced by it. But the essay's conclusions are not explicitly theological and should, hopefully, be credible to non-Christians.

To date, those conclusions have been expressed in one way. Christianity's public witness should be with, within, without or against the governing authorities depending on the respective moral orientations of the gospel and the area of the state within which it seeks to operate.

But they can just as easily be expressed the other way round. The statute book should reflect Christian political values and the Church should be permitted to partner with the state if, and only if, Christianity can articulate (and realise) a vision of the public good that actually persuades the public. In other words, although this is running ahead of ourselves with examples, the presence of bishops in the Lords or church schools or army chaplains or state-funded Christian welfare organisations will depend on whether, by doing what their Christian faith compels them to do, such groups contribute to the public good in a way that the public recognises, accepts and desires. If the public is persuaded, these phenomena will be legitimate. If not, their continued operation in their existing form would constitute an unacceptable privilege.

Rowan Williams has made a similar point, with specific regard to how "Christian" a nation's laws should be:

> The degree to which law will reflect specific views and convictions grounded in religious or ideological belief will vary from one society to another, depending on all sorts of factors - most crucially on whether a group is thought to have persuaded a credible proportion of the population at large that such and such a policy is just or desirable.[2]

Whether or not you agree with the logic that leads to this conclusion, the conclusion itself should be capable of commanding consensus. For secularists, it will mean showing that the Christian vision of the good is not what the public wants or that, even if it is what it wants, other, non-Christian groups, can deliver the goods more effectively, more efficiently or without any of the supposed drawbacks.

Conversely, for Christians, it will mean articulating, through public proclamation, and then realising, through public assembly and action, a vision of the public good. The extent to which this attracts and inspires the public's moral imagination (as with the Jubilee Drop the Debt campaign) or provokes political resentment (as with the 1985 *Faith in the City* report) will decide the extent to which the Church's witness is and should be "political" or "merely" public.

In reality, of course, few examples of Christian public witness are likely to provoke such obvious public support or political irritation as the Jubilee Drop the Debt campaign or the *Faith in the City* report. More will inspire *and* incense the public, ensuring that the debate over the role of Christianity in British public life continues to run and run.

The important thing is that when it runs, it proceeds not by name-calling or polemic, but by a genuine attempt to describe and analyse varying concepts of the human person and the public good, how far they are successfully realised by groups that advocate them and, crucially, the extent to which they are desired by the British public.

what would this mean?

If this argument is persuasive, it remains to be seen how the framework advocated by this essay might work. The basic position - that the nature of Christian witness in the public square should be dictated not by the desire of some for privatisation nor of others for privilege, but rather by recognition of its contribution to the public good - begs three questions, closely linked to those cited in the previous paragraph. These constitute the framework for analysing the Christian role in the public square. First, what is the moral orientation, or conception of the public good, that underpins Christian public witness? Second, how successfully is that realised? And third, how consonant is it with the moral orientation of the (part of the) public square in which it seeks to operate? The answers to these questions are unlikely to decide definitively on the role of Christianity in the public square, but they should steer us towards an answer.

1. what is the Christian moral orientation?

This essay has consistently referred to the Church and to Christian public *witness* in the singular. A cynic might justly point out, in response, that this is something of a pious fiction. "The" Church in Britain houses as wide a variety of opinions as the society in which it operates.

This is a fair point. The Church's biggest obstacle to effective public witness is probably itself: its variety of different opinions on different matters, voiced from within different traditions, with different degrees of sensitivity and intellectual depth. No large body can expect neat homogeneity, but the Christian voice in the UK can sometimes seem more like a cacophony.

> *The Church's biggest obstacle to effective public witness is probably itself.*

What, if anything, constitutes the moral orientation of Christian public witness? Is there a Christian "North" against which varied and complex moral orientations of the British state might be measured?

Given the cacophony of sometimes mutually hostile Christian voices in the public square, this seems unlikely. However, there may be an answer in Christianity's understanding of the human person, an understanding that is shared by quite distinct Christian theologies and denominations.

The Christian faith is fundamentally about relationships. The biblical narrative, from the creation and fall in Genesis 1 to 3, through the reconciliation of the cross, to the consummation of Revelation chapter 21, is that of a relationship, between creator and creation, ruptured, rescued and restored.

Relationships provide the key that unlocks an otherwise bewilderingly diverse, meandering, elusive, multi-genre biblical narrative. Man is created as a relational being, for whom it is "not good … to be alone".[3] (Genesis 2.18) The idea of covenant, on which the entire biblical narrative is founded, is singularly relational, "a bond, not of interest or advantage, but of belonging".[4] The purpose of the Exodus is not simply to free the Israelite slaves, still less to punish their oppressors, but, as the constant refrain in that book has it, "so that they may worship [God]". The Torah, the Sermon on the Mount and St Paul's ethical teachings are founded on the idea of love, a supremely relational value. Jesus' ministry reached out to those excluded from communion with God and his people, forgiving them and bringing them back into the fold. His teaching crystallised around the commands to "love the Lord your God …

and your neighbour". (Matthew 22.36-40) St Paul repeatedly describes the cross as a form of "reconciliation" with God. The Christian understanding of God as Trinity is uniquely relational. Christianity is a relational religion or it is nothing.[5]

This relational "North" informs the Christian understanding of the human person, an understanding that is shared across all mainstream denominations. John Zizioulas is former Professor of Theology at Glasgow University and King's College, London, and one of the world's leading Orthodox theologians. In his much cited 1985 book, *Being as Communion,* he wrote that "the being of God is a relational being: without the concept of communion it would not be possible to speak of the being of God."[6]

This has significant consequences for our understanding of human nature:

Outside the communion of love the [human] person loses its uniqueness and becomes a being like other beings ... if communion is conceived as something additional to being, then we no longer have the same picture. The crucial point lies in the fact that being is constituted as communion...[7]

A similar point is made throughout Catholic Social Teaching. The *Compendium of the Social Doctrine of the [Catholic] Church* records in paragraph 34 that:

A concern for relationships lies at the heart of the Christian conception of the good.

Being a person in the image and likeness of God ... involves existing in a relationship, in relation to the other "I", because God himself, one and triune, is the communion of the Father, of the Son and of the Holy Spirit.[8]

Similarly, Pope Benedict XVI writes in his encyclical *Spe Salvi:*

Life in its true sense is not something we have exclusively in or from ourselves: it is a relationship.[9]

From the evangelical tradition, the Christian think tank, the Jubilee Centre,[10] has developed a biblical social ethic that sees relationships, as articulated in the Torah and the corporate life of early Israel, as *the* unifying idea:

Relationships lie at the heart of a biblical social vision, address the core of contemporary social, political and economic problems, and provide a language and agenda which is faithful to the Christian tradition whilst also open and inclusive to those with whom we must work if our concern for social reform is to deliver real change.[11]

A concern for relationships (or "relational thinking" or "personalism" - the various terms have much in common) lies at the heart of the Christian conception of the good, and is shared by all mainstream denominations. The task before Christians in twenty-first century Britain is, first, to articulate this in as persuasive a manner as possible and, second, to show that they do, in fact, walk their relational talk.

2. how successfully is that Christian moral orientation realised?

The second question, which follows on from this, is how do you assess the effectiveness of that walk? Assuming that the public, in the form of its elected officials, is persuaded of the desirability of the relational vision of the good as articulated by Christians in the public square, it remains to be demonstrated that that vision can be realised in an effective and efficient way.

There are obvious difficulties with this. First, what precisely is relational health? We may instinctively recognise a good relationship, but it is less easy to identify what precisely fosters good relationships within society.

Second, how do you measure relational health? Any number of proxies might be used: levels of trust, community knowledge and participation, self-reported well-being, or, inversely, absenteeism, crime, family breakdown, debt, income inequality, drug and alcohol dependency. But these will only ever be proxies.[12]

Third, how can you be sure that it is Christian public witness, as opposed to some other social factor, that is making the difference in any given situation? Cause and effect is notoriously difficult to trace in complex social situations. The various proxies listed above are liable to be influenced by any number of factors. How can we be sure that Christian public action is making a difference?

Such difficulties may sound insurmountable, but they are no more problematic than those faced by attempts to assess trends in, for example, social capital. Indeed, in some instances, the analysis is likely to be comparatively straightforward. "Faith-based" enterprises dealing with drug addiction or debt, for example, will have specific objectives that can be and are measured with a degree of accuracy.

In other cases, like hospital, army and prison chaplaincy, evaluation will be more difficult. Few doubt that the pastoral care offered by such official chaplains does an enormous good - even Lord Harrison acknowledged that. But how much and how "efficiently" (if the word is not too coldly econometric) is not always clear.

Still more amorphous phenomena, like the presence of bishops in the House of Lords or Establishment itself, are effectively unmeasurable. Valid arguments may be deployed relating, for example, to the way in which the bishops form a concrete link between life in their diocese and the business of the second chamber, or the way that Establishment, whilst undoubtedly a relic of an earlier age, may yet do more social good than an unknown and untested constitutional arrangement, reached through a process of what is almost bound to be a politically messy and socially divisive compromise. Counter-arguments can be made equally validly. The presence of 26 Anglican bishops in the House of Lords, for example, is anachronistic and anomalous, given the size of the actual worshipping Anglican community in Britain today and the presence of other faith groups in society. [13]

Such arguments are unlikely to be conclusive, and may not even be persuasive, but they will nevertheless form the basis for any debate on such large-scale, historically-rooted and socially-complex issues.

3. how does that realisation fit with state conceptions?

Assuming that the relational benefit of Christian public witness is both well-articulated and well-realised in the public square, it would still not follow that it should or would take place in partnership with or within the governing authorities. It is quite conceivable, for example, that a particular Christian understanding of relational health would sit ill-at-ease with the state's, thereby invalidating partnership.

Such was the issue at stake when the government clashed with the Catholic Church over its adoption agencies in early 2007. The Christian conviction that children need both a mother and father conflicted with the government's new equality legislation, leading to a much-publicised stand-off in which Catholic adoption agencies were given 21 months to adjust to new regulations or face closure. Despite the fact that everyone recognised the supremely high quality of the work conducted by the adoption agencies, with their proven track record of placing often traumatised children with good families, the conception of the good that the agencies were working to - that children need a mother and a father - left them in tension with the state and facing the withdrawal of official sanction, which, in this instance, meant closure.

It was disagreements of this nature that led people, from very different ideological positions, to recognise a nascent anti-Christian inclination in government policy.

Thus Cardinal Cormac Murphy-O'Connor said, rather regretfully:

> I begin to wonder whether Britain will continue to be a place which protects and welcomes the works of people shaped and inspired by the Church. [14]

Whilst secularist AC Grayling wrote, rather more triumphantly:

> When individuals cannot allow their religious loyalties to be trumped by their public responsibilities, they should resign.[15]

It is worth emphasising that tensions of this nature need not come only from one side. One of the many remarkable things about the Iraq war was the near-unanimous Christian response it provoked. The Archbishop of Canterbury and the Cardinal Archbishop of Westminster issued a joint statement casting "doubts … about the moral legitimacy" of the war, as well as its "unpredictable humanitarian consequences", and virtually all English bishops opposed the invasion. [16] A number of army chaplains travelled to Iraq with the troops, in the pay of the Ministry of Defence. As with their hospital and prison colleagues, few doubted the enormously positive impact they had and have, on young men, women and their families who found themselves in the most frightening and stressful situations. However, their presence as Christian pastors cannot but have been made difficult by the morally unconvincing origin of the conflict in which they found themselves. Were the government to engage in military activity of the moral dubiety of Iraq again, the continued presence of Christian pastors working in an official capacity with the troops might become problematic.

These examples of adoption agencies and military chaplaincy point to the complexity of the issues at hand and the need for careful, case-by-case analysis. In most cases, that will involve assessing Christian and state conceptions of the good, but in some a third, clarifying factor may be integrated.

That factor is public opinion in its rawest form. The classic example of this is church schools. The debate over church and other faith schools takes place in the often unspoken but surely decisive context of overwhelming public support for such schools. The fact that parents queue up to send their children to church schools, with some atheists even being willing to lie about their beliefs to get their children accepted, surely points towards popular approval of what it is that church schools stand for. That popular approval is not available in most other cases. The public does not tend to get a chance to vote, let alone with its feet, on the success or desirability of faith-based organisations' debt counselling or drug rehabilitation schemes. In such instances, its opinion is mediated and represented, with varying degrees of accuracy, by elected officials. But in those instances where the public's actual moral orientation is so in evidence, it cannot be ignored.

conclusion: "doing good"

Ultimately, the role of Christianity in the public square of twenty-first century Britain will depend on the extent to which, by doing what it must do, it can persuade the public that it is "doing good".

In 2004, the world's most famous philosophical atheist, Anthony Flew, announced that he had changed his mind. Three years later, he published a book explaining his decision, simply and provocatively called There is a God. Flew's "conversion" - to deism, not Christianity, it should be noted - is not only of great interest in itself, but underscores the absurdity of those arguments that claim that "faith" should be privatised. On that basis, Anthony Flew, newly convinced by evidence, which he recognised as persuasive rather than conclusive, should henceforth keep silent in public.

The alternative, however, of failing to recognise that there has been a significant change in Britain's mental and moral atmosphere over the last 50 years, is hardly more compelling. Britain is not a post-Christian country in the way some describe it, but it is certainly not a Christian country in the way it once was considered to be. Failure to recognise this will lead to painful anachronisms and the rightful sense that the Christian position in the British public square is unduly privileged.

The answer lies neither in privatisation nor privilege. Instead, this essay has argued, it may be found in the slippery and shifting concept of the "public good". Christianity is a public religion and nothing is going to change the Christian imperative to public proclamation, public assembly, public action and, if necessary, public confrontation.

However, the precise role that Christianity plays within the public square can and does change. This essay has argued that it will and should change according to its ability to articulate and realise an understanding of and contribution to the public good that sufficiently persuades the public. This emphatically does not mean that Christians should seek to articulate and realise a contribution simply *because* it persuades the public. On the contrary, Christians must do what they understand Jesus Christ calls them to. Instead, it means that if, in following Christ, what they say and do persuades and inspires the society in which they live, they may find a role saying and doing it alongside or within the governing authorities. If, however, it fails to do so, for whatever reason, Christian witness will still be public; it will simply be without or even against those official structures.

Put another way, this means that if Christianity is to operate alongside or within the governing authorities, the fruit that it *naturally* produces as part of its corporate life will need to be "in keeping" with the taste of the day. If the taste of the day is very different from that of the Church, Christian public witness will be without or against those authorities, public rather than "political", in the sense we have been using the word. If the two are closer and more compatible, the potential for partnership will be there.

Ultimately, the role of Christianity in the public square of twenty-first century Britain will depend on the extent to which, by doing what it must do, it can persuade the public that it is "doing good".

chapter 5 - references

1 Holden, *Makers and manners*, p. 27
2 Rowan Williams, "Secularism, Faith and Freedom"
3 The force of this statement is slightly blunted in English translations. Up until this point in the narrative, the word "man" has been a translation of the Hebrew word *adam*, deriving from *adamah* meaning ground, and denoting man as a physical, i.e. biological, creature. Following the creation of woman, verse 23 uses the word *ish* for man, meaning not so much a physical creature as a full, human "person". The narrative appears to suggest that it is only in relationship with one another that humans become persons. See Jonathan Sacks, *The Dignity of Difference: How to avoid the clash of civilisations* (Continuum, 2002), pp. 150-51
4 Jonathan Sacks, *The Dignity of Difference*, p. 151
5 Although Judaism does not, of course, share Christianity's understanding of Jesus, St Paul or the Trinity, this statement could legitimately be made of *Judeo*-Christianity, as the writings of Jewish thinkers like Jonathan Sacks and Martin Buber remind us. "A person makes his appearance by entering into a relation with other persons" Martin Buber, *I and Thou* (T & T Clark, 1937), p. 62
6 John Zizioulas, *Being as Communion* (SVS Press, 1985), p. 17
7 John Zizioulas, *Being as Communion*, pp. 17,101
8 *Compendium of the Social Doctrine of the* [Catholic] *Church*, para. 34
9 Benedict XVI, *Spe Salvi*, para. 27
10 For which, declaring an interest, the author previously worked
11 Michael Schluter and John Ashcroft (eds.), *Jubilee Manifesto: A framework, agenda and strategy for Christian social reform* (IVP, 2005), p. 19
12 For thoughts on this see Michael Schluter, "What charter for humanity? Defining the destination of development," Cambridge Papers, vol. 15, no. 3, September 2006
13 See Andrew Partington and Paul Bickley, *Coming off the bench: The past, present and future of religious representation in the House of Lords* (Theos, 2007)
14 Cardinal Cormac Murphy-O'Connor, "Religion and the Public Forum"
15 AC Grayling, "Prejudicial concerns," the *Guardian*, 22 October 2007
16 http://news.bbc.co.uk/1/hi/uk/2782509.stm Perhaps this is not so surprising given how far short of the traditional Just War criteria the invasion fell